CW00470578

AT THE VERY END
OF THE ROAD

PHILLIP J. EDWARDS

Whittles Publishing

Whittles Publishing Ltd.,
Dunbeath,
Caithness, KW6 6EG,
Scotland, UK

www.whittlespublishing.com

© 2021 Phillip Edwards

ISBN 978-184995-497-6

Epigraph taken from The Hill of Summer
reprinted by permission of HarperCollins
Publishers Ltd. © 1969, JA Baker.

Printed in the UK by Page Bros (Norwich) Ltd

There is no mysterious essence we can call a 'place'. Place is change. It is motion killed in the mind, and preserved in the amber of memory.

J.A. Baker, *The Hill of Summer*

For Jo, who has loved this place with me and has loved me for a lifetime.

CONTENTS

Stirrings – On a Soft Day 1

The Place – At the Edge 7

September – The Surreptitious Changeling 17

October – Swallowed by Sunbeams 35

November – Where the Curlews Call 51

December – Mud-dancers 67

January – Wings of Supplication 83

February – Unabashed Vivacity 97

March – The Wrong Side of the World 113

April – A Hole in the Sky 129

May – A Filigree of Music 145

June – Monsters on the Stairs 161

July – Cogitations of the Divine 177

August – A Field of Dreams 195

Epilogue – An Outsider 211

Acknowledgements 215

STIRRINGS
ON A SOFT DAY

Beyond the marsh with Friesian cows chewing cuds in buttercup-strewn meadows beside rhynes[1] thick with yellow flags; over the bump and across the common to the sea; past the sand dunes and the higgledy-piggledy Hebridean fences; through the hamlet and around secret bends heavy with the scent of hawthorns; past chicken sheds redolent of ammonia, and a chocolate-box cottage; at the very end of the road. We first saw the Farm on a soft day in July – grey and damp, the air heavy with fine drizzle as if sifted through the muslin of the clouds above, a gaunt Bronté-esque dilapidated collection of buildings with horses grazing the front garden and a little owl whirring across the adjoining field to land abruptly on a lichen-spattered barn roof. The house stood proud, in defiance of its neglect, flaunting its treasure for all to see despite its tarnished visage. Oh, and what a treasure; its location – set between the gleaming river and the silver sea, forgotten by time, and with an inestimable potential for wildlife. In that moment, unbeknown to us, it took our all and clamped itself to our souls.

In reality, we knew we never had a chance, for it had sucked us in through a haze of deceptions – for a start it was already sold, and when we drove away we convinced ourselves that it was too big a project, unaffordable, and just as well that it had been sold. We had arrived that fateful day as the result of a long, long search. I had become bored with the ecological desert of the gently rolling fields that pass for hills in the eastern borderlands of Cambridgeshire. I meticulously searched the Sunday newspapers for something different every week, something unusual, something where I thought we would feel at home. My wife, Jo, came to dread Sundays, when I would announce with barely contained excitement that I had found a watermill in a Welsh valley,

---

1   Rhyne: a drainage ditch – rhymes with 'green'.

a croft on a Scottish island, an abandoned farm in the west of England. Each Sunday she would gently let me down – it wasn't practical, it was too far from any airport for me to make my overseas work trips. So the weeks became years; although Jo was happy, my restlessness reached boundaries I couldn't begin to describe. We did make a couple of trips – once to a lovely ruined farmhouse nestled in the hills with spectacular views of the Black Mountains, and once we even flew to Scotland to look at the dowager's house built into the corner of a four-acre walled garden on the Duke of Argyll's estate, close to Wigtown Bay with its rusting Second World War Mulberry harbour. But none was quite right.

The particular Sunday I found the Farm in the paper, Jo had run out of rebuffs and counter-arguments. The advert said 'adjacent to a nature reserve and Ramsar site', and my heart flipped. What was an advert saying 'Ramsar site' for? – the vast bulk of the population would have no idea that this meant a wetland of international importance for birds, but I worked with Ramsar sites regularly – and with that, the magic started to weave its spell. When I called the estate agent, I was crushed to find the property had already been sold but something made me persist and I was told there was nothing to stop us looking at it – from the outside. So for some unfathomable reason we made the trip across the country to view an already sold, derelict farm – from the outside. Four months after that soft day, after a string of coincidences that had me seriously contemplating the concept of destiny, it became legally ours. Twenty months later, after significant renovations, we moved in.

Since then, some nineteen years ago, whenever I have been at home I have wandered the footpaths and the lane and the fields beyond the house two or three times a week in all weathers and all seasons and all times of day. The area of land is tiny, less than a square kilometre in total, and yet it has exerted a pull on me out of all proportion of its size.

I have been lucky enough to have walked the surly bonded earth[2] and trodden many foreign fields far from England's shores and seen a hundred things you have not dreamed of. I have ridden a pony above the vertiginous valleys of the forbidden kingdom of Mustang high in the Himalayas where snow pigeons swirl and fall in flurries; seen ships marooned in desert sands

2 See *High Flight* by John Gillespie Magee, Jr.

of what was once the Aral Sea; heard a thousand larks sing in the dawn above the grass steppe of eastern Mongolia, and eaten dates and frankincense honey beneath the dragon's-blood trees on Socotra Island in the Arabian Sea; listened to the music in the endless wind of Patagonia; and watched a million painted ladies migrate across the Anatolian plateau. I have marvelled at condors soaring above Andean volcanoes and albatrosses shearing the winds across the Southern Ocean; seen macaws paint the light above the waters of the Amazon basin, and gemsbok trudge the world's highest dunes in Namibia; watched cranes' courtship ballets in the icy mists in the demilitarised zone of Korea, and platypuses swimming in Australia's shaded streams; and observed the translucent form of a white hawk slip through the dawn light amongst the ruined temples of Chiapas like the reincarnation of a Mayan god. I have viewed dinosaur footprints in the folded sandstone of Tajikistan, and swum with turtles in the Celebes Sea; gaped in awe at the dances of the birds-of-paradise in New Guinea's rainforests; stepped amongst the penguins on the snows of Antarctica; and sat at the edge of the world above the seabird cities on the fog-shrouded cliffs of islands in the Bering Sea. Yet despite all this, it was this tiny area of western England that claimed my heart on that soft day twenty years ago. When we arrived, we arrived to die here. The Farm became our sacrificial idol, and on its altar we laid our future – everything we owned and far more besides; things we could not even begin to imagine. Yet in return it has granted us a peace beyond everything it has demanded, transcending the commitment of energy, thought, deed, and above all money, to leave us secure in the knowledge that we had found our place in the cosmos. For us, there will never be another place. It is the magic of this place that draws me over and over again to walk and to watch, to step each time anew with excitement and anticipation for each time it shows me something new. It is this that I wish to share.

So, what is a place? The dictionary[3] defines it as 'a particular point or part of space or of a surface, esp. that occupied by a person or thing' and as 'a geographical point'. But for me, a place is made of memories, single or multiple. Certainly, its physical geography and history are key determinants of what is here in the present, and I have outlined these in the next chapter to provide a canvas on which to paint the rest of the book. Yet to me the

---

3   Collins. www.collinsdictionary.com

largest part of a place, that which defines it, are the moments that we experience while present. Have you noticed that when you return to a place it is never the same? Your memory of it has fixed it like a photo or a video. It is a snapshot to which you can never return to because the place constantly changes and your memory of it has been filtered through your emotional response to it. A beach, say, at sunset will be different from the same beach on a rainy morning; as it is different at high and low tide; and as it is different if you are sharing it with the love of your life, or alone and grieving a loss. It is still the same place geographically, yet it is different. But what of a place that is full of memories, say one where you have spent twenty years? The best descriptions enable a reader to build mental pictures of the subject. But like the beach above, such descriptions are usually singular and hence provide just that snapshot. But what if the place is described a hundred times? How much closer would that bring a reader to capturing its soul?

There is in modern nature writing a generally accepted view that in order to supply the all-important connection between author, subject, and you, the reader, some sort of narrative, some framework of human emotion, is required to provide it with a rationale. I contest this. To me it is simply an extension of the long-held Western vogue for placing humans at the centre of everything. For me, the place is all – not the people inhabiting it or visiting it. Once television wildlife documentaries focused wholly upon the wildlife, yet many now seem to be simply vehicles for non-biologist celebrities to act as presenters. Similarly, the concept of 'getting close to nature' is a contradiction perpetuated by those who do not know it, for the best you can do is to let nature get close to you – if it wills it so.

Nature comes with patience. So this book is in part an experiment. It attempts to translate tight visual observation of intimate details of wildlife and landscape from this tiny area of western England into sensuous literary pictures through lyrical imaginative language. The writing proceeds slowly because nature happens slowly, changes are gradual. Sometimes nothing happens; if exciting things happened all the time as television would have you believe, then the exciting would become mundane. Sometimes things repeat themselves. Hunting and feeding occur often in the text, but then Woody Allen's[4] view that 'Nature is … like an enormous restaurant' carries some truth. There is no story save that of the slow but eternal change of

---

4   Love and Death.

the seasons, no narrative connection of journey or emotional restoration, no focus on a single species, no discussion or allusion to the environmental issues of our age, no characters. Indeed, there is barely any mention of humans at all. Yet in attempting to remove the 'me' from the pages of this book, I face the inevitable conundrum that my presence is a constant – they are, after all, my observations and the ensuing prose is intensely subjective. Yet my aim has been, to quote Melissa Harrison writing of Oliver Rackham,[5] to 'intrude in a personal way into the text barely at all', and if you find what I have written interesting, to paraphrase L.C. Miall writing about Gilbert White,[6] it will be because nature is interesting, not because I am interesting.

Inevitably, there are occasions when my emotive response to a scene or event is the key to its being. In those cases, I have taken the difficult decision to deliberately use anthropomorphism, not because I believe in applying human emotions to animals – quite the opposite – but as a mechanism for projecting that personal response to the scene without introducing me into it. So should you choose to read on, there will be no handrail for you to hold, nothing to lead you from one section to another; no literary link. The book will take you through a year, beginning in autumn, for that is the natural start point here, the season when the wind begins to blow and brings the birds south. I have eschewed a diary approach or a description of a day; instead I have provided eight vignettes in each month, some short, some long, some single events, some combined from many years apart, that together attempt to capture the elusive soul of this place; those intimate moments with the birds and the landscape and the weather and the sounds and the smells and the passing seasons of a dozen fields, some saltmarsh and a boundless expanse of inaccessible mud – each one 'killed in the mind, and preserved in the amber of memory' – each one adding to a sense of place at the very end of the road. Whether that experiment is successful will be for you alone to judge.

---

5 *A Living Landscape*: Melissa Harrison on Oliver Rackham, *The Illustrated History of the Countryside*. Slightly Foxed magazine #43. (https://foxedquarterly.com/melissa-harrison-oliver-rackham-literary-review).

6 'White is interesting because nature is interesting; his descriptions are founded upon natural fact, exactly observed' p. xxii in *The Natural History and Antiquities of Selborne*. Gilbert White. Edited with an Introduction and Notes by L.C. Miall and W. Warde Fowler. London: Methuen, 1901.

THE PLACE
AT THE EDGE

At the very end of the road is a seven-bar metal gate. It is chained and padlocked, and marks the exact line where the tarmac stops. Beyond it the unmetalled track continues, ruler-straight with ninety-degree dog-leg bends. If I stand looking over the gate the farmhouse lies to my left, its stark visage now softened by the addition of wooden shutters. Two hundred metres from where I stand, and directly behind the house, is the sea – at least when the tide is in. To my right, seven hundred metres across two fields, is the river. Ahead of me, and just over a kilometre as the curlew flies but a bit further for me since I will have to follow the track, is a rounded sandy point where the river curves into the sea at the apex of the bay. Within these distances lies a roughly triangular area containing twelve fields bounded by flood protection banks; the seaward one old and indistinct but still effective, the one along the river newer and more prominent to the eye. Outward of this, mostly on the river side, is a large area of saltmarsh which from a satellite photograph could whimsically be thought of as being the shape of an elephant's ear, with the river floodbank being taken as the point of attachment to the head. Beyond the point lies a small island ripped from the peninsula by a major storm sometime around 1798 when the sea swamped the lowest lying land. This remains now as a narrow channel. Behind the island, the main deeper river navigation flows, and on the far bank of that is a small holiday resort. Dwarfing all of this, in terms of area, are the mudflats of the bay. The tidal range here is one of the highest in the world, and on the lowest spring tides the mudflats extend out perhaps six kilometres beyond the foreshore, and run parallel with the coast well past the base of the peninsula, some four kilometres distant. They are inaccessible to humans on foot, for the mud is soft and sticky, and the running tide will cover in excess of a kilometre in an hour.

The physiography of the whole of the intertidal area in the bay and the river is dynamic. The mudflats appear permanent but in fact are constantly shifting, the ribbed and swirling patterns of the ridges and furrows, and the position of the sandbanks on their surface, are redistributed after most storms by the power of the churning waves. The island has changed shape considerably since it was formed, erosion having narrowed it and accretion elongated it. Additionally, the main area of saltmarsh was once an island in the river, but natural processes and an abundance of sediment have meant that this has joined to the mainland and separated from it several times. Most recently it joined sometime between the Ordnance Survey maps of 1900 and 1919, and the old channel remains as a low point through which tidal ingress occurs today. The saltmarsh is flat and low-lying, fissured by muddy channels, and pocked by natural pools and three lagoons constructed in 1977 to diversify the habitat. They are replenished by tide and rain but dry out, particularly in summer. The grass sward is short and vivid green, close-cropped by sheep in summer and birds in winter, but is being invaded by longer sea couch-grass coming from the sand dunes along the top of the foreshore. This is a relative of the more familiar marram or dune grass, and just as sharp and spiky. The saltmarsh is flooded several times by the highest tides in most months except high summer. The rhythm of the tides influences everything here, most obviously the twice-daily covering of the mud which pushes the ducks and the waders and the gulls to roost high up on the foreshore or the edge of the marsh, but more subtly it affects the strength of the afternoon sea breeze and evening land breeze, the extent of coastal mists, and the level of the ponds in the fields, for the perched freshwater table floats above it.

The rhythm is a complex one. Twice a day the tide rises and falls, but the levels change according to the phase of the moon. At new moon and full moon, the tides (called spring tides whatever the season) are at their highest and lowest, flooding the saltmarsh and then withdrawing so far across the mudflats that they seem to have gone to foreign shores. At quarter moons this tidal range moderates so that these neap tides play see-saw only with the mudflats and do not reach the saltmarsh. Overlaying this is another rhythm, that of the seasons. The tidal range is most extreme at the equinoxes and least at the solstices. Over this another cycle is imposed by the moon's elliptical orbit around the Earth so that the tidal range at perigee (when the moon is closest to Earth) is larger than at apogee (when it is furthest away). And then there are further cycles superimposed one upon the other, emanating from other astronomical effects and largely involving the sun. Indeed, so complex is the system that Jonathan White in his book *Tides*[7] notes that 'By the twentieth century, more than four hundred [cycles] were identified, … each [having] a tidal effect.' Added to these he writes about the effects of harmonics and resonance which occur when two or more of these cycles come together. Weather adds other effects, with high-pressure systems dampening predicted levels and depressions sucking tides higher. What is of interest here is that in spite of these cycles (or perhaps because of them), the spring high tides in this area always occur early in the morning, around dawn in winter and a bit later in summer. That is when the best birding is to be had, for these tides push the birds furthest landward and provide the most intimate views. The corresponding evening high tides are always after dark in winter and at dusk in summer. As a result, I take most of my walks in early morning since this not only corresponds with the best tides for birds but, as any birder will tell you, this is the time that birds are most active. And besides, dawn is a mystical time in which it always feels good to be up and out. You will find this reflected in the preponderance of descriptions of morning in the forthcoming chapters.

The peninsula is derived mainly from maritime sediments and some river-borne alluvium. The former is the result of longshore drift whereby the prevailing current causes the waves carrying the material to break obliquely onto the beach, but as each sprawls over the beach with that energy spent, the ensuing backwash drains perpendicularly under only the influence of gravity. If you could see the historical pathway of each grain of sand or pebble it would show a zig-zag up-and-across the beach and then straight down, each cycle carrying it further and further towards the point. The original beach was shingle, and this was used to construct an unconsolidated bank to provide sea defences at an unknown date. Aerial photographs from 1946 show that wooden groynes were present to

---

7   White, J. 2017. *Tides: The Science and Spirit of the Ocean*. San Antonio: Trinity University Press.

help reduce erosion. However, by 1950 the hybrid cord-grass (*Spartina x townsendii*) that had been brought here from Poole Harbour in 1928 had provided sufficient accretion that reeds had started to grow, and there is now a large reedbed that fringes the whole of the seaward coast of the peninsula with only a few short breaks. On average it is about eighty metres wide and occupies a slight hollow between a low sandy beach and the shingle bank.

So the land here has come from the sea and has returned there many times, and probably will do so again. But for now, it is land. It has grown slowly, pushed along inch by inch, but while slow in our terms, geological time has barely had time to blink. Maps produced by the county council show that just eight thousand years ago, when Neolithic people were sharpening flints, this place was undifferentiated freshwater marshland, probably with several small islands. A thousand years later, when the first known seawall was being built to protect a village from rising sea levels, at Tel Hreiz in what is now Israel, the land here had reverted to sea and saltmarsh, the result of marine inundation that is known to have reached as far as twenty-five kilometres inland from today's coastline. Five thousand years ago, when the construction of Stonehenge had just commenced and the world's oldest living organisms, the bristlecone pines in the White Mountains of California, were mere saplings, the land here was still just sea. Although water levels appear to have receded by 700 BCE, when legend has the founding of Rome by Romulus and Remus, it appears that this locality remained sea and saltmarsh and that it stayed that way for some time thereafter. However, by 280 CE, when Britain was under Roman occupation, the reconstructed maps indicate it to be dry land in much the same configuration as today, although it would seem that this is conjecture since one hundred years later it is again shown as being sea and saltmarsh. By 1000 CE, when the Danes and the Saxons were still contesting the ownership of England, the area again appears to have been land, but with the river set on a course through the middle of the current village.

Today, this land still lies at the edge. The farmhouse occupies the highest point on the peninsula at just under nine metres above ordnance datum (effectively mean sea level) but given that the highest tides reach just over seven metres AOD, it is a delicately balanced existence. Without the sea defences most of the peninsula would slip beneath the waves several times a year. A cross-section at any point along the peninsula would show an escarpment in miniature – the steep scarp slope rising from the sea to about nine metres atop the blunted ridge of the old dune line running through the fields down its the entire length around thirty metres behind the reedbed, and the dip slope falling away very gently to the river. It also lies at the edge agriculturally, for it falls in the bottom grade – 5, Very Poor – of the government's land classification. The soil is mildly alkaline, sandy, and nutrient-poor, and the dozen fields are all permanent grass used for grazing or hay. Most recently, all have been tended with skill and understanding by a farmer in the village who worked them for over fifty years until his recent death. This place was furrowed in his weatherworn face for he spent every day outside in his faded olive coveralls. He taught me that grass becomes 'blue' after a lot of sun and 'crispy' after a lack of rain. He would move his sheep between these fields every few days to ensure the best possible pasture for them.

The history of the fields goes far, far back. There is some evidence for prehistoric occupation of the middle peninsula prior to the Middle to Late Iron Age (400 BCE–43 CE). Deposits of pottery and animal bones, and an assemblage of plant remains resulting from crop-processing and foraging, have been found. Several ditches that probably formed part of field systems suggest that around the later part of this period a more formal attempt was made to manage and drain the landscape for settlement and farming. There is further archaeological evidence of dwellings in the same vicinity in the late Roman period (250–410 CE) but increased flooding of this and a much wider area in the fourth century has left the archaeological record scant. The area is not recorded in the Domesday Book, but then the smaller estates are much less well-documented. The first direct written record to the village is from the thirteenth century, when its tenants were said to have owed rents in 'geese, garlic, and cheese', but the earliest reference to this small piece of land itself is of a manor house being present in 1584. This, and everything else along this part of the coast, would likely have been destroyed by the well-documented flood of 1607, now widely ascribed to a tsunami. This produced waves of five and a half metres in height that inundated land two and a half miles inland and wreaked havoc in thirty villages, causing death and destruction to people, animals, and buildings. Accounts state that twenty-eight people were drowned in the village directly across the river and another twenty-six in one close by. A map of 1750 shows a manor house located on the tip of the peninsula, and it may have been rebuilt on the same site as the one that existed in 1584. It was called The Warren, clearly a reference to an area abundant in rabbits. The manor became a watch house, occupied by customs officers, between 1686 and 1776, and was subsequently licensed as a public house, in 1778. Ironically, there is a story that it was then raided by the customs as a house of ill repute, but more likely for smuggling or non-payment of taxes. It was demolished sometime between 1829 and 1840 – and we have a fancy, but absolutely no proof, that some of the rubble would have been used to build our farmhouse in around 1850. The boundaries of the various estates are unknown, but the twelve fields and saltmarsh clearly fell under two landholdings. One included the aforesaid manor, while the other formed part of the rectory manor located across the river. This was owned by Balliol College, Oxford, and sometime between 1687 and 1704, a parcel of thirty-nine of its acres, located on this side of the river and likely including all or some of the area that is the subject of this book, was granted to trustees to provide exhibitions (scholarships) to the college.

The remoteness of the far end of this peninsula can be further judged by the fact that the houses at this end of the village were until 1933 part of the parish across the river. Indeed, the family who built the Farm used to cross the river by boat each Sunday to attend church service until around that date. It was only at this time that the sheep drove across the common and the marshland at the base of the peninsula (i.e. the road which the gate straddles at its very end) became a more reliable route to the outside world than the river. The drove was not metalled until 1961, around forty years from the time we moved here and several years after the first motorways in Britain were built. Yet another indication of the area's remoteness comes from the fact that the Farm is the last locality from which the white-tailed eagle (now reintroduced on Rum and the Isle of Wight) was recorded in the county – the Farm's then owner having shot one on 1 December 1945.

The current landscape is probably little different from that of times past except for the presence of the fringing reedbed. The grass fields are all traditional pasture or hayfields. Only one is used exclusively for cattle, the others for sheep but with cattle put to them at various times. Its hayfields are cut according to modern practice in June, with only one field cut traditionally in August: the latter maintains the highest floristic diversity and abundance of the twelve. Some of the fields are separated by ditches known as rhynes, and while in the past these were wet, their water levels have visibly dropped over recent years as a result of a falling water table. All fields have hedges and/or post-and-wire fences. The hedges are predominantly hawthorn and bramble, but blackthorn and elder are present. The taller trees are mostly crack willows and goat willows (or sallow) with a little introduced ash. In places, the footings of ancient walls made from beach boulders can still be seen.

The path along the coast is a twisting, undulating route along the weathered and slumped sea defence – grass for the most part, but with pockets of shingle erupting to the surface, where they crunch noisily underfoot. It is fringed by patches of dense bramble whose thorny fingers arch arthritically outward, seeking to extend their reach. Sometimes they enclose both sides of the path; in others the seaward side is open to the reeds. On the biggest of tides, perhaps once every two or three years, the lowest points on the path will hold a film of seawater. The path along the riverbank is more recent and hence straighter. Originally located along the midpoint of the three-metre-high sloping floodbank, it now follows the sheep path through the sea couch-grass, along the toe on the river's side. The lane used by the farmers to access the fields with their machinery runs along the centre of the peninsula, turning sharply around the right-angled field corners to maintain this position as the peninsula narrows towards its tip. It is gravel, pocked with holes, and grass runs along its centreline. In places it is overhung heavily by wind-arched trees and bushes.

This then is 'my place', although the reality is the opposite, for I belong to it rather than the other way around for even though the legal documents show a part of it to be mine, I will never fully own it, just occupy it temporarily, merely a transient in its existence, a fragment of its history. Yet it does not matter where this place actually is; it could be anywhere and comprise any habitats. Everyone will have a place, a place where they feel that they belong, grand and sweeping, small and mundane, or something in between. The important thing is to walk there as an outsider; for as observers outsiders we will always be, always looking in to understand, and waiting for those precious moments when one of its denizens will make eye contact and not flee but accept our presence.

So, tread softly, stand, and be silent; let go the ceaseless chatter of your mind, be still, and watch carefully, and learn not just to look but to see, not just to listen but to hear. Repeat the same walks, observe the same things, ask the same questions, and reflect upon the answers; wait and feel and let your place speak to you until in some small way you come to understand it, for only with time and understanding will it offer up its soul.

SEPTEMBER
THE SURREPTITIOUS CHANGELING

The sun shines. Soon autumn will fall out of the west on an advancing cold front, but for now the ghost of summer lingers. Just. Although the harsh heat has passed, the soft warmth of a hazy sun has dried the dew. Lethargy still fills the air; cows are sitting; a robin sings its desultory autumn song of sad regret from amongst the last of the clematis flowers climbing the cobbled walls. A hobby sweeps through the sky in an upward arc, raining calling swallows in its wake like a kingfisher trailing water from a pool. Summer drifts away in the piercing brightness. The river gleams. The fields slumber. Heat haze shimmers the blurred horizon.

Far above, high over the lush grass meadows, a buzzard glides through the warm afternoon air. Feeling a rising current tug under a wing tip, and with the merest tilt of its fanned tail, it leans back into the thermal, primaries bowing, filtering the air, muscles stretched but not exerted, wings seeking out the tenuous lift the decaying bubble provides, for on this warm anti-cyclonic day the air is rancid and yellowed with pollution trapped below the inversion layer, and the turbulence is harsh and bumpy. It circles lazily, slowly, slowly higher, until from the ground it is little more than a tiny imperfection on the blue corona of a flawless sky, an aberrant pixel in a digital photograph in need of correction. At three thousand feet, as the thermal dissipates, the air is clear and smooth, and the bird will be able to view the peninsula jutting into the chocolate mud of the bay, like a green thumb above a fist, as if raised in entreaty, hitching a ride; or, from the other direction, looking like a little Florida. The saltmarsh at its end is bright green and crinkled, fissured and edged by sweeping muddy sand where the sinuous reptilian river offers its gift of pale ochraceous sediment to the sea. The mud of the bay, exposed at mid-tide, is darker and striated in rough parallel corrugations, the result of some thalassic plough. Water glints silver in its furrows. The village huddles down behind a thick line of fringing reeds, the few pale houses and farm buildings snaking along the abstract of the road between the random pattern of the fields, while far to the west the dark purple-brown of the hills and the distant high ground of the moor form a curved horizon in the haze. The buzzard turns and glides upriver, trading height for distance and one panorama for another. It must know the lie of this land well, for it has passed several winters here, and while it may not view below from so high in the shortening days to come, it is renewing its acquaintance with the landscape after its recent return. It drifts from view, along with the fading warmth of summer.

In azure vaultless halls he lifts
On gentle updraughts, rises, drifts
Between the clouds in sunlit rifts
Exalting in the warmth

And splays his pinions to the air
The touchstone of his life, and there
Turns lazily in circles fair
Caressing thermals soft

Amongst the coral canyons climbs
Sunward, free from the confines
Of land left distant, quite sublime
An artistry of flight

And gently banking, slow, serene
Soaring high as in a dream
As sunlight sparkles off the rhyne
Its glinting meets his eye

Unwinding slowly, now he glides
Across the river at high tide
Its sensuous silver curves so wide
And melts into the blue

A gentle morning shimmers, the dew refracting spectra in the meadows. In the tall grass and hedgerows, a thousand spiders' webs droop under the weight of crystal inlays, their intricate beauty laid bare, their deadly purpose rendered redundant. Single strands of gossamer stretch in gentle curves, vaulting the chasm of the path like the support cables of a suspension bridge and begging the question as to how the spiders sling them across the seemingly unfathomable gap between the brambles. The river flows silver under flat pewter skies, the clouds layered pale upon each other like Chinese watercolour hills, the distant knoll rising from a crinoline of mist around its base. The distant power station is gilded by the opaque early morning sun, rising out of the morning sea mist, squat and heavy like a golden Buddha in meditation – or the centrepiece to a rock concert, the dry ice all around, the first riffs of the bass guitar reverberating silently in the mind. Beside it, another is being constructed, a second place of worship to the great god of power, the gaggle of cranes squatting over it like Gerald Scarfe caricatures of flamingos or storks.

Shelduck are flying again, their black and bottle-green remiges having been replaced by their annual moult. Numbers in the bay are falling as they disperse from what has been their home for the last six weeks, but squadrons still sortie east along the coast on stately wingbeats, encouraged by an equinoctial spring tide to find higher roosts. Over the flooding saltmarsh, the shrill clamour from a thousand black-headed gulls sounds like shouted accusations. As the sun breaks free of the cloud, the soft-silvered land transmutes to blues and golden greens. A reed warbler creeps furtively through the base of the reed stems, gleaning insects from the vegetation, occasionally snapping with deceptive speed at those flying by too closely. It rests on a stem at the edge of the reedbed and preens, bending its head down to riffle its bill through its pale breast feathers and extending a wing to nibble those on the underside. It creeps away through the base of the bed only to reappear moments later at the top, turning side-on to sunbathe. Sunlight dances in the wet cornea of its brown eye. It turns its head away and the gleam dies. It drops back into the depths of the dank reeds.

A hard clicking sound emanates from the shade beneath an ancient wind-pruned elder, where moss grows thick on an old wall now largely covered with brambles. A lesser whitethroat emerges, underparts scrupulously white, mask dark and smudged, its demeanour flighty and shy. It flits up into a blackthorn heavy with sloes, a fine white bloom dusting the deep purple of the fruit, deftly picking insects from amongst the thorns, fattening itself for its journey south. It balances delicately on the twigs before darting sharply back into cover, tail edges flaring white, chastening a dunnock which scurries mouse-like in the lichen-scaled branches below. Four garrulous jackdaws grub for food on and around the grazing sheep. These are patient and docile as the birds stand on their backs and extricate insects from the depths of their fleeces, but object by shaking themselves forcefully if the birds pull at their wool too hard. A buzzard sits atop a dead branch awaiting thermals, quietly surveying a party of eight yellow wagtails feeding intently while wreathed in the misty exhalations pulsing softly from the muzzles of the grazing cattle. The air is warming, the dew is drying, the spiders' webs will soon again be invisible … and deadly once more.

Dead calm. Sound carries, a distant curlew's melancholic slur as clear as a nearby wren's staccato trill. The coolness of daybreak is sharper and lingers longer now into the depth of the morning, a chastening reminder of forthcoming change as autumn probes the dying summer. As the morning sun warms, the thick white mist retreats to the river, burnished amber on top by the early sun. The landscape emerges like a print from developing fluid, slowly gaining definition and substance. The moon is fading into the frosted blue sky, barely an impression like feather dust on a window after a bird collision. Everything glitters as the remnants of the mist cling in tiny drops to blades of grass, leaves of bushes, and spiders' webs alike. A rabbit spooks across a field, its white tail bouncing amongst a myriad of rainbow shards. Hoverflies walk lethargically over the brambles seeking the perfect place in which to rid themselves of the night's debilitating chill.

Summer has been seduced by the southern sirens, for migrants abound. Along the coast path, a strange brownish bird gives a momentary view as it flies down from a bush and sets the pulse racing. For there on the shingle at the edge of the grass, nonchalant, like a trespasser claiming a right to be there, is a wryneck; a woodpecker yet not a woodpecker, reptilian in look and gait. It seems to crouch, bending its head down from its neck to feed, shuffling forwards hesitantly. It is intricately marked; lilac-grey upperparts and browner wings with pale mottling, black stripes down the centre of the crown and back that seem soft-edged as if wet dye has bled, and pale buff underparts with fine dark bars. Its narrow dark brown mask and long creamy malar stripe give an illusion of a wide frog-like gape. Its pale grey bill is short and sharp. It arches its ruffled back feathers, puffing itself out, expanding its size like a lizard basking in the sun. It returns to feeding, its long pink sticky tongue flicking out snake-like to catch ants amongst the pebbles; a breath visible as a puff of condensation in the cool air from a particularly sharp exhalation. It is wary, pausing frequently to scan its surroundings, careful to look upwards, once displaying its owl-like ability to swivel its head completely around from whence it gets its name. It works methodically along the path for several minutes, moving from the stones onto the short grass, but flies instantly when crossed by the shadow of a passing gull.

In a nearby hedgerow, busy with blue tits gleaning invertebrates from the underside of leaves, a female redstart perches on a low branch of a contorted hawthorn, constantly dipping and flickering her rufous-orange tail as if trying to rid herself of some persistent discomfort. She is an understated bird, upright like a robin but plain brown washed with grey above, a paler, slightly mottled, breast, and a pale eye-ring that confers a look of trusting gentleness. She makes a couple of sallies to catch passing flies, but like many migrants is shy and restless, and soon flies away to the bushes on the south side of the field, one more small step on her journey from the northern wooded valleys to Africa. Above, sharp sweet whistles of yellow wagtails move south and are gone. In the brambles along the track, three male blackcaps are feeding on the blackberries, having switched from invertebrates to the abundant fruit to fuel their southward flight. They are nervous, appearing only fleetingly while calling harshly with alarm, a sound like two pebbles tapped together once, but then repeated, ever moving away. Gone their phosphorescent songs of spring, now just the urgency to flee the coming winter.

Local movements are also apparent today. With a couple of harsh 'chip' calls, a great spotted woodpecker sparks onto a branch, igniting into the verdigris gloom of a willow. Boldly marked in black and white, its bright red crown and vent bring a touch of the exotic to the shadowy olive-browns of the hedge. Woodpeckers are rare on the peninsula, where trees are scarce, but each autumn brings an immature dispersing from its natal woodland, seeking its own place to settle. They rarely remain for long. It moves up the bough in a series of vertical hops, its strong toes clinging tightly to the bark between each bound. It stops hopping and begins to tap at the trunk, listening to the sound of the wood. Suddenly, with its body braced by a strong angular tail, its head blurs as it hammers and chisels at the soft wood in which it has detected prey. It extricates a beetle larva then takes flight again, looping along the hedgerow before flaring up into another distant willow. Rhythmic tapping follows it.

The dawn chill, the steady rain soaks all. In sleeked willows, a yellowed leaf detaches and spirals down. More will follow, to be ripped from their moorings by coming gales or brittled and burnt by frost, but this is the first, a quiet harbinger. Yet with that single leaf, the world has altered, a Rubicon moment, and that surreptitious changeling – autumn – has supplanted summer. In bramble tangles along the coast path, three migrant whinchats are chased by a resident robin agitated at their unexpected presence. It seems that wanderers are ill-received wherever and in whatever form they may occur; perhaps the distrust, the perception of threat, is an inherent part of being an owner; or the jealousy of the fixed towards the freedom of the traveller, the antithesis of place; or just an innate preponderance to persecute nomads. Nearby, with wings and tail spread wide, a female sparrowhawk flares to land in the tangled intimacy of an elder, shuddering to a halt, a jagged motion as the energy of flight discharges into the branch. She is set upon immediately by a magpie. Turning sharply, she glowers at her assailant through dimly glowing eyes. A stand-off develops, the magpie loudly chattering its flamenco phrases, the hawk refusing to move. Reinforcements arrive with the magpie's mate, but the hawk, stubborn, continues to resist her bullying tormentors even when one sneaks in close and pecks at her tail. But the incessant din eventually becomes overwhelming and she launches into a long low glide which, interspersed with a few powerful flaps, carries her to the luxuriant solitude of the walnut tree.

September is walnut season. The big old tree is heavy with green-skinned nuts, drying, turning black. It was planted behind the farmhouse maybe to mark the start of the twentieth century. Scratched and faded sepia photographs show fresh-faced smiling men loading hay high onto a horse-drawn cart with a sapling at the side of the stone shed which its roots now seek to undermine, but the photographs bear no dates, so none will ever really know; forgotten days, along with the forgotten people who inhabited them. One or more grey squirrels arrive at this time, looping up the driveway or across the fields. Where they come from is a mystery since they are not seen anywhere on the peninsula except at this time, and the nearest area of even light woodland is several miles distant. Even more puzzling is how they know that the tree is here and that the walnuts on it are ripening. Yet each year, come they do. But they make no attempt to indulge in the behaviour that they have passed their name to; squirrelling the nuts away into a cache is not for them. They simply feast while they can, as if they know they will not be back in winter. They have competition from the magpies and carrion crows who form a near constant procession, taking nuts from the tree or scavenging windfalls from below. They chisel off the black drying skin with heavy bills, then with mandibles opened to the limit they carry the nuts to the garden and neighbouring fields, walking around carefully, looking this way and that, often pushing a nut into several places before finally selecting a storage point, pulling the vegetation and loose grass to cover it … then back for the next one. That the birds have good spatial memory is evident by the shells that appear regularly on the grass through winter, having been retrieved and emptied, and although shrivelled and decaying walnuts are occasionally found in crevices in the barns and sheds, there are very few walnut tree seedlings in the garden and fields the following spring.

In the stillness of mid-September, the soft sunlight burnishes bronze the turning leaves of the hawthorns, the ripening berries shine casting a vinous haze across the bushes. The recent showers and increasingly chilly mornings have cleaned and sharpened the air, clearing away the cloying sweetness of summer. The quiet is broken only by an occasional robin's liquid song slipping through the willow leaves wetting them with sound. In the gentle glow of the sun, everything exudes calmness as if trying to absorb the final warmth of summer. An emperor dragonfly cruises low over the brambles, its fretwork of wing-veins like that of stained-glass windows but holding only uncoloured panes. The last of the year's green-veined white butterflies sip at succulent blackberries hanging heavily on branches either side of the path. The undersides of their wings are suffused with sulphur and marbled with blue-green like stilton cheese. Flowerless curving maroon briars, heavily armoured with an array of sharp backward-pointing spines, arc from the bushes, marauding across paths and gaps, curving earthwards, seeking contact with firm open ground in which to root and extend the coverage of each bush. The hawkbit has gone to seed, only the yellow flowers of the sow-thistles remaining. A brown orb-web spider with a white cruciform marking on its swollen abdomen trips across the silken threads of its circular snare in the tall grass to administer its lethal injection to a trapped beetle.

All around the alchemy of the seasons is evident. The birds that have bred here are leaving; those from further north are passing through. The reeds, turning rich ochre once again as the lush green of their leaves ebbs into the rootstock, are alive with sedge and reed warblers; the brambles with whitethroats feeding amongst the perfumed blackberries. The southward wave is building; none will remain much longer. The sedge warblers 'tchack' harshly as they flit from stem to stem, their broad cream supercilia prominent in the mellow sunlight, their plumage dark and wet from the dew that silvers the reeds' leaves, weighing them down. Reed buntings sit atop dead stems, feathers scruffy and subdued; they are deep in moult, for they are not migrating and will see the winter through here. Many swallows are already southbound, streaming steadily north-east throughout the morning, following the leading line of the coast. Once they have crossed the river, they will again turn south. They flick low across the fields and hedges with shallow-beating wings, a direct and urgent flight taking them away from the shortening days and cooling temperatures, such resoluteness contrasting with the carefree aerobatics of a handful of their locally-breeding congeners still skimming over the fields reminiscent of summer. The flashing white rumps of two house martins are with them, a stockier species seen here only as passage migrants.

At the point, each piece of driftwood is adorned with a southbound wheatear, like mascots on car bonnets, or the latest must-have fashion accessories. Warm tawny, bright-eyed and alert, they perch before dropping onto the heavily-cropped marsh grass. They feed amongst the grazing sheep, bouts of fast running interspersed with pauses as the birds bow to pick drowsy crane flies from the sward. They pump their tails rhythmically, intermittently jerking downwards on their legs with convulsive spasms as if jolted with electricity. They fly back to their perches, their white rumps magnetic to the eye. Beyond on the mudflats, the first pulse of dunlin are busy refuelling for the next leg of their journey. Amongst them, an early grey plover in remnant breeding plumage embellishes the beach, its silver-spangled cloak drawn tightly about its mantle, its ermine-edged black waistcoat fraying with autumn moult. Nearby, two knot are much less regal, their rufous finery reduced to tatty remnants, their fresh winter plumage more advanced. Overhead, a greenshank towers southward, its trisyllabic whistle ringing behind it, a sound of valediction.

Light crawls into the equinox morning from the west, weak and insipid, seeping over the land through the first gaps in the massive clouds of the trailing edge of the storm. In the east, clouds are ruched so thickly that there is no sign of the sun and no colour in the dawn. The wind has battered the peninsula and far beyond all night, lashing the house and trees invisibly in the darkness as the storm has drifted slowly eastward. It is the first big one of the winter season, accorded a name beginning with A by the Meteorological Office to designate it as such, and it has blown away the last vestiges of the mirage of summer. Daylight brings no respite as the wind hurls itself across sea and land. Black-headed gulls stream seaward to feed on the mudflats vacated by the ebbing tide, tossed and buffeted yet defiant in their course. The receding sea turns from tarnished silver to ochraceous grey as the morning ages, and colour bleeds into the landscape. Blue sky is spreading from the south, slowly wiping away the clouds, but to the north the rain still hangs as frayed umbilicals from menacing plumbeous cumulus, tinged lilac at their bases. In the east, pale yellow sunrays leak through the clouds illuminating the naves of wet air. On the mudflats, the waders have all turned to face the relentless wind while continuing to feed as yet another squall brings slanting rain thrashing across the surface, the streaming sheets stretched pale and condensed dark by the gusts like some monumental barcode. Over the reedbed, a frisson: an erratic jinking flight discordant with the wind becomes two birds – a hobby hunting a skylark. The falcon's flight is taut and responsive and fast, but even it cannot predict the turbulence sufficiently rapidly to fly the skylark down, and it gives up. Their flight paths part as the lark seeks refuge on the ground behind the reeds and the hobby turns out across the shore, its fiery orange thighs glowing dully as it banks.

Onshore, all is in motion; hawthorns and blackthorns tremble uncontrollably, willows sway and weave, reeds toss, grasses stream. Incongruously, the wind will bring green back to the peninsula for a few days as it rips the weakened yellow leaves from the branches, littering them on the ground in the lee of the trees and bushes. Small land birds are confined to dense shelter. A wheatear, surprised from a small patch of shingle amongst the brambles, jolts upward to perch on an exposed briar, tail pumping and body bobbing rapidly and awkwardly as it seeks to maintain its balance in the pummelling wind. It remains close to the watcher, its fear innate yet somehow uncomprehending, as if the wind has dulled its recognition of danger – or perhaps its fear of uncontrolled flight in this wind is greater still. It drops out of sight on the far side of the bramble bush. Butterflies have vanished from blackberries. Dragonflies no longer patrol the lane. Yellow dung-flies have forsaken cow pats. Gates fret on their hinges. In the fields, sheep graze in opposition to the waders, backs to the wind. They sport patches of blue dye on their fleeces indicating to the farmer that they have been tupped and should bear lambs next spring. The only bird evident amongst them is a single magpie, its head ravaged by unseasonable moult, and although its eyes are bright and shining, its unflinching lack of fear bears the quiet desperation of disease. In the lee of a dense willow copse, decorated with crimson rosehips, there is a surprising oasis of calm. There, an indefatigable robin sings sweet sorrow unseen from deep within a bush, where all else there is only the song of the wind.

Scudding clouds uncover the sun, sending shadows racing north unhindered by the gale. The land shines. The saltmarsh is empty save a few shelduck at the edge of leaden pools whose surfaces, lustred by ripples, are like decorative hammered metal. The distant sea is a neon tube of motion between the melanoid mud and the stygian clouds beyond. As the next rain shower passes across the sun, a rainbow germinates behind it, growing tentatively at first before blooming confidently into full maturity, a flaring empyreal rift arcing perfectly across the blackened sky, corralling pale, sun-drenched cloud within its inner violet band while its red outer forms a barrier to the wild, dark vapour raging beyond. And then above it, in those barbarian skies, a perfect reflection, red inner, violet outer, glimmers and grows, converting the outer skies to the light, leaving only the area between the two a dark heathen place in which the rain-reflected light fails to shine. On the horizon where the two arcs ground, the nebulous form of the holm lies in the gap between, veiled in the tresses of the dark clouds. Slowly, the whole optical artefact fades into obscurity shifting as the rain moves east, gone from this viewpoint but forming elsewhere for other eyes. On the mudflats, the birds are oblivious to its presence. The wind has increased, the rain lashing the surface of the mud, spattering particles into the air as each impacts. The shelduck have ceased feeding, hunkering down hiding red bills under wings. Gulls stand into wind, heads bowed to their breasts. Only the waders continue to feed. The squall moves through, foreshortening the horizon, wrapping the pools and the mud and the sky in hues of lavender-grey. Yet in minutes all changes again, the sun reviving the palette of this landscape, the long flat lines of blue and brown and tawny and ochre and green. Distantly, another rainbow rises from the sun-drenched sea like a geyser, fine white sequins of rain glittering in front of it; the rainbow fading into the fuliginous sky as this rain that gave it life arrives to fall from overhead. The shelduck that were almost invisible on the distant shadowed mud just a few minutes ago now gleam marble white with the sun's return.

Mid-morning and the cycle of squall, sunshine, rainbow continues, some rainbows enduring, some fleeting, some full arcs, some constrained between the sea and the clouds above. Yet slowly the clouds become scarcer, the showers more infrequent, until the sunshine prevails and the transparent clarity of the light brings the far distance near. Only the wind remains.

High tide, sepia waves still surging shoreward on the inertia of yesterday's gale, still rolling with threat and menace, spray still scattering from their crests despite the decreased wind. Low over the sea the white rump of a Leach's storm-petrel, a storm-blown, pelagic wanderer, winks in the gloom. The tiny form flutters weakly, legs trailing, tiptoeing on the heaving waters like a deity, picking items daintily from the heaving surface. It dips and rolls and bobs, the random path of a piece of windblown litter, and yet it is resilient enough to have lived its life far out in the North Atlantic. It drops into troughs, disappearing like a ghost-bird, seemingly inevitably caught and pounded by the waves each time, yet always re-emerging on its erratic path, legs down, pattering the water, forked tail spread. Rarely seen close to shore, storm-petrels are even nocturnal at their breeding grounds and for a reason – great black-backed gulls. But that scourge is in the bay, a hulking form driving over the foaming breakers on long, immensely powerful wings, its sallow eyes locked on to its prey. It dwarfs the waif. The gull's huge yellow bill opens to snatch the petrel from the air but at the last moment, the petrel dodges, the gull's head turns following and the bill snaps shut on empty air. The petrel climbs above the waves, flicking strongly, the fluttering flight abandoned. The gull rolls hard right, driving once more after its quarry. The gap disappears, the gull strikes, and the petrel dives below the breaking crest of a surging wave, too low, too dangerous for the gull, which overshoots. The petrel climbs once more, turning seawards. Again the gull turns tightly, but the pursuit has alerted others to an opportunity for food and several smaller herring gulls have converged upon the scene – no organised cooperative hunting party this, but a group of voracious selfish individuals; winner takes all. The great black-back is no longer in pole position, but its stronger wings draw it quickly back to the flock. The lead gull moves to grab the tired petrel but it banks clumsily to avoid collision with a browner, younger, bird intent on making its own attempt, and once more the petrel tumbles towards the churning surface. The flock wheels and follows – the petrel climbs, but preoccupied by the chasing pack it crosses directly into the course of the great black-back, straight into its gaping bill like a billiard ball into a pocket, or an insect onto a windscreen. The gull drops to the heaving water and plunges the feebly flapping petrel below the surface, holding it firm until it detects no further resistance, then raises its head and swallows the drowned corpse in one gulp. It rises and beats downwind towards the shore; the trailing flock forlorn – winner taken all.

Summer now frets at the edge of memory for one morning deep in September amidst the lengthening shadows of autumn, chill ahead of the first frost, and with the sky the palest of china blues, the swallows have gone. The sky is empty and stilled; the air is quiet, the twitterings ceased, a void now born. The green warmth of summer is now a dream away, long in the past and far in the future. It awaits their return. Along the lane, the willows' yellowing leaves are rusting around their edges. In the rhynes the willowherb is blown, the opened seed pods recurved and matted like tousled and unkempt tawny hair, white down scattered across their tops. Hedge bindweed drapes from the lower branches of the hawthorns and smothers the brambles along the banks, but it is withering. Its blowzy white trumpets remain, but they are crumpled like discarded crinolines. Thistledown drifts. The dead leaves, killed in the spring storms, have been shredded and torn from the windward side of the hawthorn hedges by the early autumnal gales while those in the lee remain largely green.

A communion of long-tailed tits follows-the-leader along a hedge, invading a hawthorn and startling away a dunnock. Eight dainty balls of black-and-white-and-candy-pink feathers, they search the bush meticulously, picking at curled dead leaves, holding them with one foot while using their tiny beaks to prise hidden insects from within. All the while, extravagantly long tails work feverishly to maintain balance. They look like miniature soft toys and hang like Christmas tree decorations. An effusion of faint sibilant and soft rasping calls maintains constant contact between them. One bird leaves and flies to a nearby bramble bush, but the foraging remains good in the hawthorn and the others linger, forcing the pioneer to return to the flock. Only several minutes later does another bird fly to a blackthorn studded with sloes and follow-the-leader is reprised as the flock dips across the path and the unceasing search for food goes on.

The coastal reedbed, empty of birds, has fallen silent. The warblers have taken their conversations south to Africa: just the rustling breeze remains, singing of separation, the sweet smell of humid decay pungent in the air. At the reedbed's edge a pair of stonechats, plumage muted by recent moult into brown and buff with soft orange breasts, flit from ochre stem to ochre stem like a faded sepia photograph from yesteryear. They are newly returned from their breeding grounds up on the moors to the west or the north, and will spend winter along this short stretch of coast. They make repeated sallies from the tops of brambles to catch insects now lethargic in the cool. A robin, belligerent as only robins can be in autumn, takes issue with their presence atop its favourite elder, hounding them relentlessly until they withdraw. Yet curiously it pays no attention to a male reed bunting, attired in fresh streaked-brown plumage, that emits thin plaintive whistles from the same perch. Having successfully evicted the stonechats, the robin appears to celebrate possession with prolonged rapid ticking interspersed with subdued phrases from its winter song.

In the meadows, the last of the migrant yellow wagtails snap flies from around the feet of the sheep. They will be gone in a day or two. Around the pastures the eternal battle between corvid and raptor ebbs and flows. A pair of magpies aim their harsh castanet chattering at a female sparrowhawk as she comes to perch on the exposed branch of a stunted hawthorn at the edge of a field. The hawk glares at them as they fly up from the grass into the neighbouring bush, but she is in no mood to battle wills today and immediately takes flight again, slipping fast and low over the pasture. The magpies follow briefly. It is strange how the magpie mirrors the hawk's shape with short round wings and long tail, yet where the hawk is sleek and fast and powerful the magpie is slack and slow and weak. With the threat from the hawk extinguished, the pair land to feed, long tails swaying from side to side like metronomes as they walk jauntily through the grass, the deep blue and green sheen of their glossy black plumage lustrous in the autumn sunlight. Above them, the tables are turned by raptor attacking crow: below one of the small cumulus clouds that have blossomed on the weak thermals created by the midday sun, a raven soars in wide languid circles, wings outstretched and wedge tail fanned, harvesting the lift. It calls, deep expressive baritone croaks laden with the hollow resonance of an oaken barrel. Gradually rising, it finds its idyll shattered from above as a kestrel plunges from the same thermal in which it too had been soaring, now minded to drive the outsize corvid from its airspace. It stoops and rises sharply in repeated mock attacks, flapping in its dive more like a hobby than a peregrine, its agility easily able to keep it clear of the raven, which rolls combatively onto its back to fend it off, now cawing bellicosely. The raven attempts to retain its presence in the thermal, but the kestrel is not to be denied and increases the ferocity of its attacks, striking the raven twice on the tail and wings, gone each time before the raven can retaliate. The raven concedes the battle despite being twice the size of its assailant; it simply lacks the capability to win such a hit-and-run encounter with a more agile adversary, and drops from the thermal, flapping heavily away towards the river.

OCTOBER
SWALLOWED BY SUNBEAMS

You can see the wind on the peninsula; it is in the very fabric of the landscape – the stunted trees and lopsided bushes, the curvature in the reed stems, the restless ripples in the grass, the white horses running free across the waves, the ever-changing cloudscapes and shifting light. It is remorseless and wearing, but it brings the birds and chases them. Morning is bright: a weak October sun shines from between the fish-scale cloud of a mackerel sky, the herald of change. Lapwings, those rounded ushers of autumn, have returned to the fields. Fresh from the north, dunlin are uncoiling brilliant strands of silver inscriptions into the sky, twisting back and forth, rippling, reptilian, purling into brown shadows nearly invisible against the sea, then turning sharply as one on a pinpoint, a communal convulsion becoming blindingly white, exploding like a firework against the dark sky. And the wind rises. Overhead, the plovers' plaintive musings mourn, undulating on the breeze, drifting in and out of the ears as insubstantial as the braided flocks from which they come. A goldcrest emerges from the depths of an archaic elder, legs splayed between two twigs, hissing its sibilant hesitations. Its yellow crown flares briefly in the gloom. A robin trills its elegiac ode to summer from an elder heavy with purple berries. From the base of a willow encrusted with yellow lichen, a Cetti's warbler blasts out a burst of his explosive song, hurling the notes into the air. Skulking deep in the vegetation, shyness overcome momentarily by inquisitiveness, he gives a fleeting view of bright eye, cocked tail, and incongruous pink legs, then scuttles away, burrowing down into the safety of the tangles. And the wind rises.

Low over the fields, the final few swallows flee the forthcoming storm, like fragments of nostalgia migrating to the deepest recesses of memory. Three white-fronted geese labour west over the shoreline into the gale, looking for the skein they have already lost. A female merlin relinquishes the air to seek shelter in the lee of an old brick barn, fervid power barely contained within her diminutive body, volatile, an avian reactor on the edge of detonation. Inside the barn, where ferns grow lush in the damp shade of its broken roof, a wren flits and bobs and jerks on rubber legs, knocking the rain drops from the fronds as it forages and snatches morsels from the stems. And still the wind rises. The tempest, now at full velocity, will blow all day, into tomorrow and the day after. But it is itself silent; it is those earthbound things it touches that are vocal – the walls that whistle, the slate and iron roofs that clatter, the doors that whine, the windows that rattle, the trees whose leaves are shredded that creak and groan, and the sea that pounds along the shore that roars. High above, in silence beyond all hearing, the clouds chase their shadows across the sun-dappled land and sea below.

A myriad of shelduck stand sedately on the highest land haloed by the morning sun. A foam of gulls rolls along the front of the tide, scavenging amongst flotsam lifted from the grass by the rising water. Across the saltmarsh, a carrion crow caws repetitively from a fence post, its coarse grating calls carrying far over the chill pools, an ebony shaman chanting its incantations into the grey wind, its tail fanned and body convulsing as it shouts out its spells. Beyond, a fox, lean with youth, trots confidently across the marsh, its gait interspersed by short bouts of canters. Its movement is fluid, but along a narrow ridge of grassland that separates two pools it hesitates, seemingly disliking the water. It steps gingerly, placing its paws precisely to avoid wetting them. It reaches a narrow channel but is reluctant to cross, instead turning sideways along the edge, searching for dry passage. The river, ever widening as it fills, finally overtops its banks and the tide noses out over the saltmarsh. Water pours through channels, drifts across pools, and slips over grassland, transforming the green to a glittering silver sheen as it mirrors the sky above. The fox is now forced to wade through the tall stems, stopping occasionally, perplexed over its first experience of a large spring tide that is making shrinking islands of its home. As the flood all around deepens, each step becomes more precarious. Suddenly it misses its footing, falling into the cold water. It swims strongly but slowly, necked stretched out, nostrils held high, its tail floating like a giant rudder. It half-emerges onto the opposite bank of the channel where progress remains difficult, the water too shallow for swimming but too deep for easy walking. It struggles through the tall tussocks, finally reaching higher ground where only its paws are covered, then shakes itself vigorously, pulses of rolling muscle sending coronas of silvered spray blooming into the sunlit air around it. Then a sudden discovery – it is not the only refugee on the saltmarsh; there are other smaller ones that should make easy prey. It stops, head tilted questioningly, nose twitching, ears cocked, sensing food. Wet fur forgotten, it gathers itself, drawing down on its haunches, poised, before leaping in a flowing rufous arc and diving snout first into the base of the long grass, its front paws landing immediately afterwards, cushioning remaining weight falling from above. It has missed. Again it leaps high into the air, jack-knifing along its spine as if hit by an electric shock, agile and twisting tightly as the unseen small mammal seems to try and pass underneath it. It chases around skittishly, seemingly random movements interspersed by weak pounces, but these too result in failure, the initial surprise lost and the invisible prey too elusive now to be caught. The fox perseveres, ears constantly moving, snout sniffing, nosing around in the tall grass like a wild pig rooting out acorns, but the water is slowing its movements. After a while it gives up and begins the slow trek landwards. Close by, four little egrets watch it carefully, their usually ceaseless pacing interrupted, their necks craning until it passes safely by, when their methodical stalking resumes.

Dawn is pallid and sullen and windswept. The clouds are massed and rounded, hulking stromatolites, brooding, and sagging with rain. The wan sun rising behind them washes the merest tint of pale almond through the sky. Along the coast path, abundant droppings in discrete latrines mark the boundaries of badgers' territories, the spoor rich and dark and full of pips from the blackberries on which they have been gorging. All is in motion, a million silvered reed-heads waving in unison, the dark tangles of brambles tossing, and the bare branches of the hawthorns and willows knocking and creaking. The sea is a diseased brown, flecked once more with the putrescence of the gale. Over it, a line of black-headed gulls hugs the swelling surface in buoyant flight, one behind the other as they progress into wind. The leaders frequently swap positions by rising into the stronger wind above before dropping back where they rejoin the line like team pursuit cyclists on a velodrome track.

On a drift log on the saltmarsh a male peregrine hunches, perched on one leg, the other held close to its belly in a knotted fist. His head scans constantly, seeking a target to quieten the hunger that will be gnawing in its belly. He slips into flight, sleeking low across the saltmarsh, seemingly frictionless like water over the windscreen of a moving car. Accipiter-like, he hugs the contours of the marsh, barely rising over the ridges and low embankment, wing tips flicking the tallest grass stems, until shooting free over the lagoon he jolts a thousand waders from their roost. Panicked wings roar as they strain to distance themselves from the elemental menace that has just shot bodies full of adrenalin. Ignoring all, he hurls himself over the sea couch-grass to ignite another eruption of waders, this time from the beach. Shrill alarm calls drown the sound of the breaking waves. He banks sharply, now uninterested, curving back low once more over the stunted dunes and across the lagoon where some twenty shelduck and curlew have remained standing, watching the falcon's progress as if experience has taught them that it will not take birds on the ground. He climbs hard, and the reason for his provocation becomes apparent: far above, his mate drifts on extended wings, feeling the fronds of the cloud base. She has been waiting for the opportunity to stoop that has not yet come – a suitable alignment of prey and height and wind and light that has not quite been realised.

He sideslips deftly underneath her, rising on the other side to join her neatly in formation. With each making only the smallest of adjustments of their wings to counter the gusting wind, they hold station high over the agitated waders on the shore. Minutes pass before the male half-closes his wings, dropping with dazzling speed. The curlews blaze from the beach in a frenzy of wings. He tilts in amongst them, flapping strongly, attempting to tease one bird clear, but despite a few half-chances, he never quite succeeds. He rises high on stiff wings, re-joining the female, who has remained above. Again, they wait for the waders to settle nervously, before this time trying together, the female leading, dropping in a rapid glide through the blizzard of hysterical wings, trying hard to isolate a single individual, but with the same unsuccessful outcome. They circle away from the palpitating wader flock, then come in as one, low over the shore, rowing hard into the wind, jerking the flock back into the air, tormenting it, ever angling to prise one bird loose. The male almost succeeds, closing in tightly to a curlew, reaching his leg out to almost brush its back, panicking it into a sharp turn away from its congeners and into a terrifying empty space which the female suddenly fills, twisting tightly in pursuit. But the curlew dips at the last second to avoid the life-ending impact and gets lucky with the arrival of another straggling group of curlews, merging into the safety of its numbers. Undaunted, the peregrines regroup and reprise their manoeuvre, passing through the first flock too quickly, teasing the second to no avail, and resorting to blind power surging through the third, trying desperately to rake a victim from the multitude. Still they fail to make contact. They leave the shore aflame with activity, a trail of displaced birds and whirring wings. Frustrated, they make an impudent pass at two great black-backed gulls sitting on the strandline, surprising one into reluctant flight on lumbering wings – a predator now momentarily the prey – but the other stays fixed, turning its head to ward off its would-be assailant with a disdainful snap of its beak. Outwitted or unlucky yet still hungry, the peregrines finally depart, low along the shore towards other distant wader roosts, to try again.

Evening grey curtails a day of low skies, the still air silky, the sea like lustred steel. Redshanks' gentle whistles are muted in the tranquil cooling, the sound of the distant waves barely audible across the glistening mud. Over the flooding river, three hundred avocets wheel in a straggling line, fluttering over the water's edge as they attempt to land though each time seemingly repelled by the rising water. They lift again in a beautiful monochrome ballet of pied wings flickering in exquisite motifs over the metallic water. The delight here is not in the changing colours and shapes as in a dunlin flock but in the hypnotic repetition of pattern in the avocets' wings pulsating together, the birds stretching into filaments as they circle back out over the river. They never do find suitable ground and instead turn away upstream touching down mid-river in front the blunt form of the church tower just emergent from the trees on the far bank. They are one of the few waders that swim readily.

A curlew heads towards the point, calling its long ringing vibrato, the gentle rise suddenly curtailed and descending sharply, hanging tremulously in the stillness, a sound filled with infinite sadness for things long departed. Beneath the heavy leaden clouds and veils of distant drifting rain, the fire of an autumn sunset spills a deep copper glow across the fields like an open furnace door radiates the gloom of a foundry. The sun sinks below the horizon, the door shuts, and as the Earth's shadow closes out the light, a little owl yaps like a Pekinese into the chill darkness of its dawn. Lapwings, returned for the winter, now call unanswered questions into the moonless sky. Across the fields their slurred whistles rise like hope through the darkness; fearful and fragile, each seems to be retreating, shunning contact with the ear, from the first moment that it starts its ephemeral rise up the scale and through the air, untouchable like frost, melting away even as the ear first notices its existence.

The sun rises over fields flooded white from the river, archipelagos of dark bush tops floating where once there were hedgerows. The morning mist has stolen the horizon. Soft wet calls of lapwings float above the veil as small flocks search for lost fields in which to feed, their loose laconic flight like tissue blown in the wind. The mist rises slowly, like a half-forgotten thought searching again for the surface of consciousness. As it does, the fields re-emerge, but the promise of the morning slips away like the promise of summer into the chill autumn air. The glory of the dawn sunshine tarnishes; cold grey replaces warm blue. Colour leaches from the landscape as the mist transforms into cloud, soaking up the light from the sky and absorbing the shadows from the land. Overhead, many skylarks are moving just below it, a steady trickle of small flocks, their presence marked by thin calls drifting on the wind. A silvered dew-soaked field is scarred by a dark trail from the recent passage of a fox, the moment of its passing fossilised until the dew dries or the rain washes it away. Along the coast, the reedbed is ragged after a recent storm, slumped and spent, silent and still. Beyond, mud sinks under the rising lustre of the incoming tide. Along its creeping edge, weaving strands of dunlin ripple as the water pushes them slowly shoreward. Uncertainty courses through them, a bedlam of pulsating piping voices that ceases immediately each time they surge in earnest from the shore and recommences each time they return to scurry over the mud, feeding frantically, a life of constant motion, an urgency about all.

Two days after the full moon, the peak of this month's highest spring tide has now flooded the saltmarsh. The near riverbank is barely defined, a fragile broken line of grass between the river and the flooded marsh; now a place where the land has become water, and the water has become drowned sky. In a pool, a group of lapwings huddle with their feet in the clouds, the ripples retreating from their legs tickling the grey sky making it shiver. A flight of teal, the males with slick oily heads, shatter the mirrored calm, lancing it upon landing, fracture lines and fragments spraying across its shining surface. Moments later their reflections join them, coalescing from the myriad of splintered shards like a video of the landing in reverse. Further out on the same pool, a group of shovelers swim, their silhouettes distinctively flat as if somehow they are hugging the water, trailing V-shaped ripples in their wake. Little egrets gather at the tidal races where the rushing water speeds white through the bottlenecks between the marsh pools carrying fish and shrimps. They take up their positions in advance of the water arriving, like anglers along the riverbank. Twenty years ago, they were newcomers here, but they have watched the tides and each other and learnt the best places to feed, gathering in anticipation at those points just before the water starts to flow, then as it slows moving onto the next link in the chain. They know the tides too, for on neap tides, when the water does not flood the saltmarsh, they do not come.

Along the coast, the mud has long been extinguished and strings of curlews are winging in to roost amongst the silken pallor of the sea couch-grass. Flocks of dunlin are trying to land amongst them, but the grass is too long for their short legs and once again they whirl into the air still searching for a safe refuge, twisting turning rising falling stretching folding, uncoiling brilliant strands of silver into the sky; leaderless, the exquisite patterns of organised chaos. Upriver, another flock ripples in self-doubt, torn between land and sky, and behind them another, while above the sky is braided with ribbons of redshanks and plovers swirling in the silence imposed by distance. Each tiny island of grass that remains in the still-rising waters plays host to a crowded tumult of refugee waders packed tightly into shrinking space. Landward, a large area of nearby saltmarsh remains unflooded where space is unconstrained, but being nearer to dry land it remains unused, eschewed by waders adhering to some ancient litany: 'Thou shalt not forsake the edge for the edge is sacred unto you.' This is mirrored closer to the coast where a large dry lagoon remains empty until the tide breaches the sand dunes and percolates through the low points to spill silver slowly out across the sand. Only then do the curlews, which have been huddled in the last of the grass or circling overhead, arrive to use it – yet even then, all congregate only on the slowly expanding film of wet, only the presence of water allowing them to feel safe.

There is always frenetic energy about an incoming tide, the constant movement of the water as it covers the marsh, flotsam surfing the channels, birds running ahead of the water or shuffling and hopping as it rises around their legs, then an eruption of flight through a flock and its associated choral descant. Yet at slack water it almost seems as if there has been a collective sigh of relief. Birds can now move at their own pace rather than that dictated by the sea. Commotion stills, clamour diminishes, waders settle and sleep. Even the water starts to slip surreptitiously away. In the quiet, a single redshank's call rings through the drizzle, decaying with the same fragility of sound as comes from tapping a crystal glass.

Two hours later and the river is redefined, land has resurfaced, and gradually the landscape is reclaiming its lost identity as water continues to pour from the lagoons to the sea and from the plateau of the marsh over cascading waterfalls into the mud canyons of the riverbanks below, each like a miniature Iguazu. Waders have woken, ducks are flying, the foraging imperative of following the moving tideline has reasserted itself, as it will do now until twelve and a half hours hence, when the next high tide will force them all to roost again.

Unease stalks the first light over the marsh; the curlew roost is empty, shelduck hold their heads high; two hundred knot parade in slow motion in the shallows of a lagoon like toy soldiers in step, first one way then the other, half of them suddenly exploding into the air on the back of one bird's misplaced febrile angst, fleeing across the flooding grass to the river while momentarily later the other half cleave away to the coast. The object of their consternation is perched upon a post surrounded by the rising tide: a male peregrine. He has clearly been hunting, though he shows no sign of having killed; for a long while he rests, placid and impassive, but as the rising water comes perilously close to the tip of his tail, he lifts. His reflection dives away into the depths of the flooded marsh as he graces the air above. He rises from the dimness of the saltmarsh and circles once out over the river; ascending now on rhythmically pulsing wings, passing the face of a single burning frond of vapour caught in the sunlight of the autumn dawn. Free now of the cloud hugging the horizon, higher and higher he climbs, up into the plaintive piping of the plovers raining from above; ever rising into the light, a bird-moth drawn towards the eternal flame. He sets his wings and slips into an easy glide, then accelerates rapidly, wingbeats now fast and flickering. He closes quickly over a line of dunlin lancing upriver and trims into the familiar barbed arrow-shape presaging a stoop. He drops vertically. As the distance between the two vanishes, the dunlin flock balloons with lost cohesion as the waders veer and flare away from the onrushing falcon, leaving just a single one to make a final last-second jink to safety as the peregrine sweeps past. Unfulfilled, he skims out across the fields, over the dunes and reedbed, flying in lazy undulations, half a dozen wingbeats lifting him a hundred feet, then a long descending glide to hug the contours of the land again, the whole repeated several times. He flies with assurance and purpose, flight taut and economical, appearing to be hunting opportunistically, looking for easy prey. Having disturbed nothing, he turns seawards and climbs tenfold, his heavy hunched shoulders powering his wingbeats. At a thousand feet he unfurls into another glide, circling tightly in front of the chromatic arc of a stunted rainbow compressed between the low dark cloud and the hills below, the violet inner band drifting in and out of vision with the unseen changing facets of the distant rain shower. His immaculate white underparts, barred narrowly with black, gleam against the plumbeous backdrop each time he swings into the rising sunlight. Slowly with each circle he drifts downwind across the peninsula, back towards the river, to be swallowed by sunbeams and showers slanting from the base of the clouds.

Dark pewter stains the horizon, the morning clouds low and soft, the tops of the eastern hills invisible below them. The holm lies dark and foreboding, remote in the sea like the listing hulk of a shipwreck; dimensions lost with distance. Above, behind the frontal system that brought the overnight rain, the clouds are puffy and lighter yet with an air of raggedness about them like much-loved well-worn clothes fraying at the edges. The air is moist and heavy and surprisingly warm in sheltered places, but October's reminder is sharp where the chilly wind prevails. In the bright but intermittent sunlight the wet fields glow vivid green and the soil a rich dark umber, but in the trees autumn dances vibrant yellow, a sacrificial beauty laid upon an altar to the wind which will soon shred it at its leisure. Briars shine with scarlet hips. It is a day of abundant meadow pipits, bathed rich olive in the sunshine, their migration interrupted by the night's rain. The flocks remain confined to the hedges and pastures, dipping and flicking from perches all along the lane. Occasionally individuals lift from bushes as if to resume a journey, squeaking in short fluttering flights before returning, still reticent to leave. A late swallow struggles southwards, chasing a summer long past and fleeing the claw of winter now close behind. Is anxiety rising within it as its food supply dwindles? Does the journey ahead appear increasingly daunting? What strange decision or twist of fate made it stay so late? A female kestrel hunches on a fence post, reticent to fly and heavy when she does, her crop bulging with a recent meal. A roving band of tits draws a few greenfinches and a chiffchaff with it as it rolls along the hedgerow, flustering robins sequentially as the activity passes through their territories. Snails are active in the damp, sliding imperceptibly over leaves and branches on glistening trails of silver mucus, each with eyes held aloft on stalks that individually retract sharply when touched by a windblown leaf. Their intricately whorled brown and ochre shells are carried at rakish angles like berets.

On the coast, the soaked reeds are dark and green and slick, rustling mutedly in the westerly breeze. Beyond, the patterns of the sky and clouds are rendered in light and shadow on the remaining expanse of the mud, as the flooding tide corrals the distant shorebirds landward. Among a group of lapwings straggling closer in along the shore, a golden plover gleams yellow in the shadow of a passing cloud; yet when the sun returns it seems to be swallowed by the brightness of the mud. The saltmarsh is almost empty save a group of great black-backed gulls sat low in the grass, two mottled brown immatures amongst them. A pair of peregrines is present – the female perched on a small post preening, heavy and thickset with a tawny wash across her upper breast, her crop heavy from a kill made earlier in the morning; the male petrified to the drift log to which he is so often a part, smaller, and more compact, with a greater contrast between his whiter underparts and jet-black head. A little egret stalks methodically through a pool, its white plumage bright in the deep shade of the grass bank. It stabs repeatedly at its reflection following it through the still water, each time breaking it into a thousand facets, yet it cannot rid itself of its presence. It runs a few steps as if trying to break free from its stalker and lunges again as if to kill it, yet the result is the same until it leaves the shelter of the bank and passes into the wind-rippled water beyond where its pursuer cannot tread.

Late October slips away. The first frost has flowered under a tender blue sky; a proto-frost, barely a frost at all, more like hard dew, it steals the colour from the leaves, muting them, making the green grass grey. The river steams beneath the rosy eastern skyline becoming amber with the gathering day. The sun breaks through the horizon's surface tension, momentarily gilding the bare branches of the trees on the far riverbank, as transient as the lustre on raw silk. A cow coughs, its breath smoking in the cold air. Ribbons of lapwing ripple over fields. A robin sings autumn from a bush, a fresh falsetto like water trickling into a well, hesitant and dripping with uncertainty, bright with hope yet eclipsed with poignancy. Distance is indistinct with the lamina of fields and trees and hills layered away, each paler and fainter than the next until merging into the sunlit haze of the horizon. Over a flat calm sea, five thousand dunlin flitter, more like flickering light and shadows than birds of real substance, a shimmering amoeba planing down to settle along the tide's edge like an excrescence of salt crystals. A short contrail from a plane flares briefly like a dying meteor. The urgency of a flock of redshank's pinging calls contrasts starkly with the serenity of the sea's susurration.

High over the shoreline, a female peregrine, rakish and lustrous in the autumn sun, turns on a wide axis. She drops a wing and sideslips on the wind, and pandemonium breaks out below. Birds convulse into the air from stationary slumber to flight in one fluid movement, a blur of wings, a crescendo of calls. The beaches empty; the sky fills, the forces of specific attraction winnow birds into monospecific flocks – boldly pied shelduck on powerful wings, their red bills shining like emergency signals; tarnished yellow golden plovers, bullet-shaped, climbing fast with rapid wingbeats into the blue; bill-heavy curlews, slow and steady in straggling lines over the sea; dunlin glittering in clouds, weaving long trails into dense flocks condensing as they double back on themselves; knot in tight fast flocks heaving seaward; grey plovers with black axillaries, compact and strong, hugging the shoreline. But it seems it's only a feint to produce that reaction, just because she can, a playful reverie, for she makes no attempt to stoop at those individuals desperately clawing at the centripetal heart of the swirling flocks below. On flickering wings, buoyed by the breeze, she climbs away into the void, leaving beating hearts and racing pulses to slacken as the flock returns to the shining mud below.

On a fence post by the coast path, a buzzard mewls repeatedly, a cat-like noise, high-pitched, drawn out, descending. It is warm brown with paler, barred underparts. Its hooked bill is a strange delicate pink with a dark tip. It is calling its impotent defiance at a second, darker, bird that has supplanted it from the part-consumed rabbit carcass lying on the short grass of the old dune line where the warrens abound. Myxomatosis is rife this autumn, the bright eyes of several rabbits already dulled by the hideous swollen pink pustules that bring blindness and a lingering death. The buzzards will feed well for a while. The disease comes in cycles here, taking four to five years to spread from the base of the peninsula to the point, ravaging rabbit numbers as it goes. By the time it has decimated the population at the point, numbers have recovered at the base and the virus starts its gruesome journey once more.

Late October is fly season, the increasing chill triggering movement from the farm animals in the fields to the houses and barns of the village. The flies come in their thousands, resting on the walls of the buildings and providing rich pickings for birds. Pied wagtails patrol gutters, picking them from the edge of roof tiles; blue and great tits take them from the cobbled walls; stonechats sally from nearby brambles snatching them from stone and air; even house sparrows join in on the bonanza. Flies that survive these depredations – and they are many – stagger sleepily across windowpanes and buzz noisily around rooms, drunkenly bouncing off ceilings and walls, looking to insinuate themselves into impossibly narrow cracks and crevices, between windows and doors, into wardrobes and cupboards and attics, there to pass the winter.

Autumn slips away in yellow
Morning mists and light so mellow
Softly burnishing the land
And dunlin gleaming on the sand
With lapwings rippling in the air
Calling calls of soft despair
For summer's done and winter's coming
Dark and cold with rhynes a-brimming
So goodbye now to halcyon
Survival's all now autumn's gone.

NOVEMBER
WHERE THE CURLEWS CALL

Days shorten, grey is enveloping, the wind infinite. At a thousand feet, a buzzard soars in loose elliptical loops amongst the frayed bases of the clouds. Sometimes it pauses, hanging over a point in the wind, sometimes it makes several loops in quick succession. It flies in a world of subdued greens and dancing greys, its available airspace gradually reduced as autumn's cloud base lowers into winter. Beyond the peninsula, the channel slices broad towards the distant world of its far shore, its waves flattened by height, its iron water scattered with ochre sun spots changing with chameleon slowness, old ones fading, new ones forming, as the clouds shift through the upper breeze. Far below in another dimension, the walnut tree, now stripped almost bare by the autumn gales, is alive with greenfinches visiting the feeder placed beneath it. Chaffinches trawl the ground for fallen seed. Great tits stage smash-and-grab raids through the finches with raw aggression, seeking sunflower seeds to carry away and hammer into submission. A song thrush, a connoisseur of fine invertebrates, cocks its head and admires a delicacy in the wet grass, disdainful of dried fast-food outlets. A stonechat bobs on the brambles nearby, alert amongst the huddled sparrows. Then uproar. Food is forgotten, cover becomes imperative. He comes fast and low, surging through the air, a solid core of pulsating muscles straining and rippling under contours of slate-blue feathers trailing a fading impression of motion behind him like a comet's tail or the light from a child's sparkler drawn quickly through the air. He flicks around the edge of the brambles punching into the tumult of citrine wings, black talons on long yellow legs grasping, striving to pluck a warm soft body from the fleeing turmoil. But not this time. The male sparrowhawk solidifies onto a walnut branch, shakes the chestnut barring of his breast, and stares back over his mantle at his flight path with vacant yellow irides, learning from his failure. He will return throughout the winter and the greenfinch flock will diminish steadily in the face of his depredations, but for now he must try elsewhere and he glides away skimming the grass field, dogged by cawing crows.

Clouds are grey and massive, the land jaded and chilled by a northerly wind, testament to late autumn's fickleness; yesterday was clear shining blue. In the east the hills are bathed in bright sunlight yet rain slants in rags across them; rainbows will be rising somewhere. Fresh out of port upriver, the dredger, bulky and angular, rides high and empty. It crawls across the empty fields on its way to gouge aggregate from the floor of the channel; a land ship struggling to break free from the grass and hedges, succeeding only as it rounds the point to the open sea. It will return, sluggish and laden like a sleepy well-fed beast, on the next high tide. On the far bank of the river, two mobile cranes in the marina are lifting sailing boats out of the water, ready for winter. On the saltmarsh, a pair of peregrines are feeding at the bloodied carcass of a recent kill. A plume of white feathers scars the green sward downwind of their plucking. Unusually, they feed side by side, heads dipping almost synchronously in a macabre parody of children's apple-bobbing, dipping to tear away flesh, rising to swallow. Yet their carefree feeding is over, for two carrion crows, seemingly naïve in their boldness, swagger across the short grass intent on easy feeding. The female peregrine rebuffs them head-on, hopping at them with wings spread, screaming her vituperation. The crows make a tactical retreat but the small distance is insufficient to allay the female's ire. She drives them further away, then turns back to her meal. The crows immediately follow, well versed in this game of tag, retreating again when she turns to attack, advancing when she attempts to return to the kill, maximum irritation their goal. They persist until the female's determination to defend her prey carries her into the air. She flies hard at them just a wing-beat above the marsh, at which point prudence takes hold and they retreat to a safe distance. The falcon swings in a low arc and lands on a low broken fence post. She rests briefly before re-joining the male, still feeding on the corpse.

Ten minutes later, the crows return, standing guard close by, staking their claims to the remains, but as the falcons continue to feed impatience betters discretion and they move in to try to snatch pickings. They continue to be repulsed whenever they get too close. Then things change. The male completes his meal, hopping a small distance away before flapping heavily up onto a nearby drift log. The female, still hungry, continues to feed, pulling the carcass over with her foot to get at as yet untouched flesh. But now the balance of power has shifted and the crows move closer. She lunges at each in turn, running with head lowered, screaming fury at her tormentors – but with the crows adopting a strategy of approaching from opposite directions, she is fighting a losing battle. Every time she chases one, the other moves in quickly to steal a beakful of flesh. Eventually she takes to the air once more, lifting the crows with her in circumspection, but this time she leaves the kill and departs for a distant shingle ridge on the riverbank. Having won possession of the prize, the crows leave it to evict a buzzard from the saltmarsh even though it is still a hundred metres distant, either from paranoia over their recently won food, or because the urge to persecute buzzards is just too strong to resist. Soon after their return, roles become reversed, for the female peregrine lands close by, standing and watching the crows feed, either still hungry or loath to leave the prey, but unwilling to try to supplant them on her own. Yet ironically the crows have wasted too much time chasing the buzzard, for the rising tide begins to lap around the kill, driving all away.

So sad, the disconsolate plovers' sorrows seep through the mists of a grey November morn. Insubstantial and achingly wistful they drift fleetingly from the clouds above and the shore below, floating mirage-like, vanishing before fully heard, illusory, a sound heard but never held. Clouds drift across the bay attached to the sea by their placental curtains of rain like tattered skirts dragging through a puddle. Light courses between their torn fabrics. Illuminated waves rear to the eyes while the distant shoreline slips away from sight in shadow. The river mouth is drained of colour, silver and sepia, slate and khaki, grey gulls, pied shelduck, only the thin strip of faded green saltmarsh and the washed umber of the distant trees bringing substance to this vapid half-land and its aqueous skies. Slack water has become the ebb, and now the world awaits the resurrection of the land. Its speed is deceptive for along the shore little movement is discernible, yet between the point and the island the river races seawards carrying thirty wigeon fast downstream, the calico-coloured forecrowns of the males bobbing bright like navigation lights in the dancing shadows of the choppy water.

Away the tide falls, exposing the glistening saltings. Shelduck arrive from sea and marsh to graze on tiny saltwater snails, while a narrow wave of movement follows the sea's edge across the shore – gulls quarrelling over flotsam, and waders feeding. Most are dunlin, trembling as if in perpetual fear, frenetic in their movement, concentrated nuclei of energy constantly skittering across the mud on blurred legs, dashing across the mud, up over the hummocks, down through the gullies, bathing in the shallows with fluttering wings, racing landward ahead of an unexpectedly high wave, then gone as one, firing into the air to perceived but non-existent danger, landing again in a flurry of wings to start over again. All is accompanied by a chorus of calls, rising, high-pitched, and slightly squeaky, merging together yet rough-edged like a choir out of tune. Their bills probe the mud tirelessly for tiny invertebrates like slightly curved sewing-machine needles but jumping from one side to the other, their progress interrupted only when dealing with particularly recalcitrant prey. Their frenzied motion is as if they are concerned that they will run out of time before finding sufficient food during this tidal cycle. Groups of ringed plovers announce their arrival with a fanfare of clipped piping. Similar-sized to dunlin, they bear no other resemblance. They are relaxed and composed, content to take a short, considered pause after swallowing each food item like Edwardian children taught good table manners, only then hurrying again with dainty steps before stopping abruptly to bow and peck at another shoreline invertebrate. With movement ceased, their bold patterning makes them surprisingly invisible, for although it evolved to break up their form when nesting on shingle, it also works well on mud where their grey-brown upperparts match its colour, their black bars mimic the shadows cast by the small hollows and hummocks carved by the tides, and their bleached white underparts shine like the reflected light from its wet surface.

Knot are present in low numbers, but even these small flocks display a propensity to huddle closely. Similar-shaped to dunlin, they are a little larger and twice the weight. They lack their frenetic energy but when they stop to probe in the mud their heads vibrate up and down much faster – the sewing machine at full speed. They run with a comic-book gait, a caricature waddle akin to that of an Olympic racewalker. Grey plovers are bulkier still; their muted muddy grey and white plumage echoes the substrate and the water around them. Rotund and stolid, they have large wet black eyes. They stand sentinel on ridges, motionless for minutes, impassive, aloof from the world around them as if pondering some distant plane. Then back to the moment when, with wary gait, they step forwards and lean for a final close inspection of their prey before dipping to extricate it from the confines of the oozing mud with their heavy black bill. When they hunt more actively, they do so with deliberation, strolling slowly, disdainful of running, taking items from a wide arc of vision, often turning perpendicular to their heading to capture prey.

Redshanks explore the convoluted surface of the mud avidly, making jerky hesitant runs interspersed by pauses to investigate areas with long pointed bills whose bases match their long vermilion legs. They disappear into unseen hollows and canyons only to re-emerge as if rising from the bowels of the earth, seeming to drag themselves from the sediment, clean, reborn, like Orpheus returning from the underworld. Largest of all are the curlews striding sedately on long legs. They progress placidly above the fevered movement below them, scanning back and forth, intermittently picking an item delicately from the surface with their curved forceps. Occasionally they condescend to plunge that improbable scimitar fully into the mud, plumbing depths not reached by other waders, to pull lugworms from their U-shaped burrows. A brief struggle, a shuffle of the feathers, equanimity restored they stride on. All will walk or run now, out across the kilometres of mud, following the tide, leaving the shoreline quiet and empty until they return, chased by the exuberance of the breaking waves.

The ragged edge of last night's rain lies frayed across the distant coastline of the channel. The storm has passed, the wind abated. Cloud hangs low over the bay, blue-black yet glowing. To the south the sky is clear and blue. The air is sharp and translucent, cleansed by the rain. Sunshine fills it. Distance is reduced. A redshank takes fright from the shore, ringing calls trailing in its wake, fraying into wind like flames into darkness. In the bay, the flat sea is a kaleidoscope of grey shot with strands of silver where the light rides the subdued swell. Above it, dunlin dance on vibrant flashing wings in tight formations, wheeling together in the sunlight. Twenty thousand wings beat as one, swirling and eddying, flashing white and disappearing dark once more, twisting in ecstatic unison, intuitive anticipation making them at one with the air, a single being cavorting in the sunlight, billowing like a silver silken sail, tumbling in the breeze, plunging in glittering cascades, stretching into trailing ribbons flickering low across the shining surface of the receding tide, folding in deep shimmering serpentine undulations, perfect sigmoid waves blinking on the oscilloscope of glowing cloud, coalescing in sweeping arcs curving shoreward, veering seaward in tightening rolls, unravelling into separate flocks chasing the wind, each swinging into sinuous streaming waves before knitting into tight clusters, re-joining, interlacing, now a single being drifting downward fluttering, falling on the glistening mud as if spent, yet resting only briefly, the exhilaration of flight bursting forth once more in renewed exuberance to shift and whirl and sparkle, the intricate flowing beauty of patterns of chaos – an avian aurora.

Is there any call in of all of nature so melancholy, which speaks so hauntingly of loss, of distant lands and forgotten times, of the wild places that frequent the remotest corners of our minds? Far, far out on the unformed horizon where the land has no right to call itself land, where it is liquefied, reforming from the sediments of the river, and the mud won't hold the weight of a man; out where the balance between erosion and deposition hovers on the cusp of accretion for now; at the very edge of the land where the waders come twice a day on the lowest spring tides to feed on the plentiful ragworms; where the birds call calls that dissolve on the wind before ever reaching a human ear; in a place of shifting uncertainties where the inability of toes to find purchase launch bouts of fluttering until the half liquid is half solid enough to tread once more …

Out on the edge of our memory,
Of the lands we can barely recall,
Where lost love is now just a yearning,
Is the place where the curlews call.

When the hurt is no longer hurting,
And the loss has left nothing at all,
There will still be a tug on the heartstrings
When you next hear the curlews call.

A place where the longing is wistful,
A brief moment on winds or a squall,
A touch on the heart beyond consciousness,
Is a place where the curlews call.

In the mists where the mem'ry grows weakest,
And the mud holds the teardrops that fall,
It is here that the echoes have vanished,
Except when the curlews call.

Stand here on the edge and listen,
For what memories remain now are small,
Over waves and through loss you will hear them,
Whenever the curlews call.

So listen and try to remember,
From the memory's dark fickle hall,
The lands and the loves that have perished,
When you next hear the curlews call.

Eight days and still the wind whines and moans as the last of a sequence of depressions sweeps in from the Atlantic. The air is unseasonably warm and moist despite its chaotic activity. Banks of dark cloud queue along the western horizon. Spindrift curls from mud-stained wave crests. The breakers collapse in foam, transferring the energy accumulated from the vastness of the open ocean to the grains of sand and granules of mud, churning them from the shore, shaping the beach for another year … or perhaps for just a day. Above, the sereneness of the gulls has been disrupted, their flight ruffled by the gusting gale and hail, their forward progress turned backward, the headwind stronger than their forward flight. Some alight upon the seething waters rather than remain in the pummelling air, a moot choice for waiting out the passage of the squall until scavenging becomes possible once more. The seaward edge of the reeds has been flattened from the wind-driven tides, the remainder still upright, writhing convulsively. In the shallow waters of the lagoon behind the splint of beach, the wind takes form as the gusts blow pressure patterns across its surface. In the bay, two great skuas toil into the wind in front of tendrils of rain slanting from clouds towering above; dark and heavy, they exude menace even at distance. Still further out against the oily sea and smoky sky are more pelagic refugees: fifty kittiwakes straggle, oscillating across the horizon, white blinking beacons casting braille patterns in the dark.

Slowly the wind diminishes. Clouds begin to break. Greyness sloughs from the landscape. Sunlight paints colours in dazzling saturation – skeletal trees russet-brown, river leaden, saltmarsh neon-green, lagoons deep ultramarine, reeds bleached ochre, the mud a rich umber. The sea turns steely-blue. Flocks of shelduck shine against the wet silvery shore. A flock of dunlin land along the edge of the dark tide. Their white bodies gleam like a string of pearls on a jeweller's brown display cushion. Abruptly they levitate again, misting the air, almost motionless, drifting on the wind, passing high over the point to the river, then slowly precipitating into denser sinuous lines that oscillate and dive, disappearing against the dark backdrop of the fields and trees of the far bank, before rising again like wisps of smoke, away to decorate some other stretch of shore. From the sorcery of the sky, a rainbow blooms over the eastern hills. Short and squat, swallowed by the dark clouds above, it refuses to be extinguished and its truncated form glows brightly in its moment of glory before succumbing to the inevitable, to be devoured by the cloud. Yet the rainbow is not done, and as the showers and light shift again, sharpening still further the colours of the land, another rises phoenix-like in its place, flaring into a full arch, polished by the rain, glowing for its ephemeral moment of prismatic perfection, then withering slowly as it too fades into the trails of the storm. Seaward, still far out in the bay, those chameleons of light, the kittiwakes, are now dark grey against the ice-blue sky and shining sea as they journey back to the open ocean.

The top of a neap tide is turning; the mud that has remained above the brown waves is full of waders busy feeding or standing roosting, the sea sprinkled white with shelduck. Tension suddenly courses through the flocks, heads turning, necks craning. A peregrine sweeps around the point pushing a wave of wigeon seaward. She is a female, hatched this year but now large and heavy and sleek, gleaming bronze in the low late autumn light, muscles rippling rhythmically as they power her wings. Waders spasm upward, the beach clearing in a moment as if some giant unseen broom has pushed away unwanted dust from a floor. She swings low across the beach, spreading her wings and tail, arcing lazily upwards over the sea, her dark-streaked white underparts glinting briefly in the sun. Wings sleeked once more, she dives back along the water's edge, gaining rapidly on a great black-backed gull, its white plumage still muddied with immature feathers as if it has spent too long dipped in the dirty sea. She rapidly overhauls the lumbering gull but slows as she passes over it, slipping easily to one side as the gull turns its heavy beak and lunges at her, as if irritated by the impudence of her proximity. She turns away and replicates the entire manoeuvre, hanging briefly over the gull with just enough distance to evade the danger held within the swipe of its beak. She retires once more. When she comes again, she does so from a different trajectory, flatter, slower, her wings more bowed and ballooning, enveloping the air beneath them. The gull ignores her this time with utter disdain, bored like a parent with a fractious child, for it is secure now in the knowledge that its much smaller tormentor is not hunting but simply using it for target practice, learning how to approach in different ways at different speeds and different angles. Twice more she comes in slowly and just above the gull, hanging briefly over it at the perigee of her orbit, then angling away. By the final time, the gull has moved too far from the point, and she heads back low along the now empty beach and lands on the opalescent mud. She preens.

Ten minutes later she lifts into the light wind and heads seaward. Shelducks paddle heavily through the waves to avoid her. She swings slowly into wind and closes over one, coming to the point of a stall directly above it, talons extended. She drops gently. The shelduck crash-dives in a shower of spray as if surprised to have been picked as a target, and the peregrine bends away, flapping leisurely, gaining height smoothly. She turns again, wings fully outstretched, and curves back in a shallow glide. The shelduck flock is now fully alert and scatters ahead of her approach, but she is fast and comes swiftly above another one, adjusting her attitude rapidly to hang just above it. It too dives to avoid her unwanted attention. But this time she stays on the cusp of a hover, waiting for its re-emergence nearby, angling quickly back towards it, then sharply upwards as the terrified shelduck dives again. She climbs steadily to a hundred feet, shakes herself in flight, sending rolls of ruffled feathers down her body like a dog shaking water from its coat, and glides back towards the mud, practising the same hovering manoeuvre briefly over a startled cormorant drying its unwaterproofed wings at the edge of the shore, as if she just cannot resist.

She rests and preens for another ten minutes and watches nine grey plovers that have the temerity to land and feed nearby. Then she opens her wings and flickers seawards again, but this time with purpose. She remains low, ignoring the shelduck flocks even as she cuts a swathe through them, intent instead on the flocks of wigeon swimming slightly further out. She angles in across the wind and comes to a hover, stationary on motionless wings angled finely enough to let the wind hold her momentarily, legs extended. The flock scatters in a storm of spray. Ducks that never dive, dive. Anything to avoid the horror. The peregrine rises and banks steeply on a tight axis and approaches again, slowly and from a shallower angle, closer to the water, her silhouette now less distinctive to the wigeon but her presence just as terrifying. And this time all the morning's practising generates the outcome she was trying to elicit: the wigeon panic and take flight. Instantaneously she climbs on straining wings, forcing the air away behind her as she wrenches herself upward. The wigeon flock coalesces, tightening even as it leaves the water, the white on the males' upper wings flashing like distress beacons in the weak sunshine. Briefly, the flock diverges from the rising falcon, but as she rolls out of her climb and dives, that distance closes like a rifle's recoil. She plunges through the flock, black talons grasping, then slows and turns but holds no prey. The wigeon have jinked away at the very last moment and now the gap between flock and falcon widens progressively. She returns shoreward, her loose flight seemingly carrying an air of dejection that failure inevitably accrues, yet only through failure comes knowledge and while her youth means she still has much to learn, the morning's experience indicates that she learns fast. She will go hungry today, but that will only sharpen her schooling. The wigeon will soon face a formidable adversary.

Early morning is flat and grey, the pink blush of dawn long gone. The fragile crust of frost on the fields is fractured by the dark pencil scribble of a moorhen's trail to a dewpond. Dark ice is incipient upon its surface.

The wind is light but the morning chill pierces all, bringing involuntary shivers. Today there are monsters on the marsh, bright blue and white with long pneumatic claws and revolving flashing orange lights and discordant beeping. All life has fled; no peregrines rest on posts, no golden plovers seep their liquid calls into the air, the shelduck swerve their flights away as they head towards the river. The monsters and their fluorescent yellow attendants working on the sluices are shunned by all.

Three hours later and mid-morning remains as dark as dawn. Bruised leaden clouds sag from the sky, leaking heavy drizzle. Greyness pervades with numbing blandness. Grey clouds over grey clouds over grey hills over grey sea; a world of monochrome layers, even the green lustre of the pastures dissolved and carried away by the cold rain. Grass is squelchy underfoot now the frost has thawed, the lane awash with mud and brimming with chains of interlocking puddles. Lapwings bleed from the sky to be absorbed by the fields as they close their wings. Golden plover – slower, more poised and balletic – step daintily, picking food items from the surface.

Starlings are restless, ceaselessly drifting over the water-logged fields in undulant flocks, each short flight heralded by a rush of purring wings. Birds rise from the rear of the flock leapfrogging those in front, the whole constantly rolling forwards like an ocean breaker, blackening the grass and hedges in a locust-like squall. They are sharp birds, pointed at both ends and with pointed wings, spiky in movement and temperament, jabbing at the ground, busy and feverish, calling continually; at distance a subdued unfocused chatter, close to a frenzy of squeaky jabbering, a wall of noise that mocks the surrounding serenity. Their presence on the peninsula in late autumn is binary – either they are present in thousands or they are completely absent, as the flocks rove restlessly across the countryside, communally exploiting the available food.

Goldfinches tease seeds from the cotton down of thistle heads, both matted in the wet. Last leaves cling to bare branches atop hedge like perching finches. Beneath one, a male blackbird tosses dead leaves energetically with its saffron beak, pausing intermittently to tweak some morsel from beneath them. It drags a small slug roughly across the ground, jerkily flicking its wings and tail and peering through narrow buttercup monocles as it wipes it back and forth vigorously through the wet grass, carefully removing the slime whose taste or texture is clearly unappealing to its palate.

Silently, a female sparrowhawk precipitates onto a low fence post and gazes around, yellow irides searing the grey gloom. A landed hawk is the antithesis of its being in flight, the body stationary and the head constantly turning this way and that, rather than the head held gyroscopically still on the flexing body; but both actions maximise the opportunity for detecting movement in the landscape. After a couple of minutes, her head locks still, body frozen with tension, gaze transfixed assessing approaches, calculating flight lines; then suddenly she propels herself forwards, crossing the field with only half a dozen wingbeats and two long low curving glides. She flips over the next hedge, startling a lapwing into the air – and perhaps herself, too, for she veers away as if surprised by the size of her potential prey. Trajectories diverge: the hawk drops low into the wetness of a willow copse; the lapwing lands in the same field but far away from any hedge and recomposes its ruffled feathers.

By late afternoon, the wind has dropped and the sea has calmed, but the roar remains in the waves, still breaking high and running long. In a world of grey and lost horizons, of glowering vapour and molten sea, an improbable alignment of sun and cloud swathes the distant holm in radiant light, a spotlight on a darkened stage. The sea and waters of the lagoon are briefly tinged violet, like an old-fashioned hand-tinted photograph. Then once again the sullen sky clamps down upon the sheer boredom of winter. As dusk descends, the soft lilac clouds release their captive sun, flooding the land with liquid amber. Far out over the dark mud, alabaster streams of wavering dunlin weave their patterns; visual echoes of the wind. Curlews' calls ripple across the mud as the western hills close over the smouldering sun. A blackbird chooks in the final shadows of the day.

DECEMBER
MUD-DANCERS

The afternoon sky is like wet slate, dark yet shining. Leaves have gone. The gnarled hawthorns and bare brambles hug the ground, trying to evade the winter winds. Everything is horizontal – sky, sea, mud, reeds, fields, layered flat one above the other. On the other side of the channel, the industrialised urbanscape leaps suddenly near from below the lifting cloud, as if by some tectonic trick its far bank has been magically transported to be but a fingertip from here; the wind- and rain-cleansed air are endowed with a clarity that dismisses distance, making the chimneys of the factories and power stations and the house-covered hillsides a startlingly intrusive backdrop to the bleak emptiness of the peninsula. Across the river, the ailing seaside resort lies shuttered. In between, flocks of waders are layered against the sky, fine nebulae of plovers high above loose weavings of lapwings above tighter sprays of redshanks and the eddies of the swirling dunlin. There is a wildness that only waders bring to a winter's sky, the vibrancy of their flight and the poignancy of their calls raining from high above that seem to pine for the wide-open places of the distant north; calls that transcend the banality of the dowdy shabby shorelines of the edge of England; the closed hotels and amusement arcades, the forest of masts of the empty yachts wintering at the marina, the squat rectangular brick buildings and metal tanks of the sewage works, the angular blocks of empty vacation apartments, the poverty of colour and the lifelessness of the windswept streets that the summer holidaymakers never quite see.

Out beyond the fields and the coastal reeds, the ridges and furrows of the mud have been conjured into limestone karst by the alchemy of the low sun. This is a place remote from us, a place we can never know, for we cannot reach it to experience it. It remains a place instilled with fear and unease; the signs call it 'treacherous' with good reason, for people have drowned trying to walk on its soft sucking surface. Only the birds find safety and sustenance here. A male sparrowhawk flushes from the fringes of the foreshore grass, plumage damp and leaden. Wraith-like, he haunts these insubstantial edges of the shadowlands, eking out an existence hunting songbirds or ambushing small waders at high tide, an enigma both fearful and feared, glimpsed but rarely ever truly seen, always retreating from the eyes that seek him. Accosted by crows and mobbed by small birds wherever he may be found, he is spurned by all, despised like a leper, an itinerant outcast exiled to the margins, passing winter shunned and alone. Short wings beating rapidly, he rises into wind before gliding out low along the foreshore, igniting a tumult of lapwings and golden plovers, fear-contagious, yet it is he who is fleeing and they who settle once more to their watchful rest.

Lean and raw, the cold and incessant wind sharpens hunger and hones survival. Five hundred curlews are hunkered down against the screaming gale on the sliver of mud between the couch-grass and the seething sea. They are tense and watchful. Bills face forwards, heads are retracted onto mantles and tilted skywards, eyes scanning constantly for the extra danger that would necessitate flight in such extreme conditions. But it comes just as they seem to know it would on this morning, a dark flickering scythe hugging the contours of the shore, a nemesis from which they can only try to flee. A thousand wings pulse the air, exploding into the turbulent vortices, bodies thrashed by invisible forces, the predicted trajectories of flight invalidated, but the urge to escape undimmed. The peregrine too is struggling, this impeccable aviator's skills tested to the limit by wind hurling spume from the wave crests, but inexorably its sleekness gains on the flock, overtaking stragglers with no further strength or ability. It rises sharply before flicking a wing over and diving the short distance back to a loose individual, raking feathers with extended talons but failing to contact the frailty of the flesh below. The curlew tumbles sideways downwind, struggling to regain flight control as the peregrine banks into wind and curves long, out over the white horses. Having made almost no headway along the shore, the curlews descend and land, grateful for the briefest respite from the chaotic conditions. They stand almost on tiptoe with wings not fully closed, on an edge, fearing to rest and fearing to fly.

The peregrine arcs back to the land, low and hard, discharging current to the shore and shocking the curlews back into the air. Slow-motion action: straining curlews at full air speed making negligible headway over the ground, peregrine at full speed making barely perceptible gain on the curlews. But slowly the curlews are drawn to the hawk, as if through some mesmeric attraction, sleep-flying into danger. Once more it draws level, reeling them in, passing beneath the flock, angling up again prior to a downward slash that never comes, for it misjudges its attitude and is flung backward; all gains of the past few minutes lost. Yet hunger drives it on, and it lowers its head once more, strains sinews anew, gives the curlews no respite. Doggedly it reduces the distance, now changing tactics and remaining low, coming in under the centre of the flock, manoeuvring like a jet fighter seeking a refuelling hose. With surprising deftness it rolls and, inverted, shoots a grappling hook skyward into the breast of the curlew immediately above it. A second sulphur-coloured hook locks into the soft warm tissue, but the prey is now a death trap, the weight too heavy, the drag too much; forward momentum lost in the wild wind, the pair tumble downwards with flailing wings. The falcon disengages, displaying astonishing prowess in the turbulence of the gale to re-establish level flight. Not so the curlew. The ripped muscles can no longer propel its uncoordinated wings. Its bill hits the waves, its head snaps backwards under it and the seething ochre monster grabs it, looping serpentine coils of water over it, pulling it down into its unquenchable depths.

Above, hunger is not yet sated. The peregrine returns, slanting in across the waves, angling in towards the flock this time rather than labouring up from behind, pushing the curlews over the shore rather than hunting them over the water, the recent close encounter with the sea too unnerving. This time the closure rate is faster even though both are in level flight, but as the peregrine reaches for the heart of the flock the curlews explode in all directions, preferring to face the heart-wrenching fear of uncontrolled flight in the tumult than extinction by rapier. Still the peregrine does not relent, each pass teaching new lessons, fermenting new tactics. It accepts a free ride from the storm, surfing downwind of the flock now coalescing again and repeats its angled approach from the sea, straight and level, slightly higher. Then opportunity from nowhere, for five dunlin in a loose line cross its approach, unaware of the incipient danger. The peregrine swerves sharply and assails them with ferocity, accelerating wings throwing it forwards as if this is its last chance. As its talons reach to pluck, the dunlin jink instinctively and the moment is lost. The peregrine sweeps by.

Hunger begets persistence. Too much energy already spent, too much knowledge of current conditions already forged, neither to be wasted. Opportunistic forays relinquished, the task refocused, the peregrine comes a sixth time across the churning waves, once again angling the curlews over the shore. The flock is now disorganised, no longer tightly knit. Some straggle in flight over the shore. For many, exhaustion prevails, the brute facts of physics overcoming even blind terror, leaving many individuals grounded even as the scythe-shaped shadow passes over them. Fatigue has permeated the falcon as well. Its muscles strain to row it forward, bringing it once more below the flock. This time all previous labour melds into this moment – a single fatigued curlew isolated from the flock and over land. The peregrine draws underneath it. The curlew emits a stream of white, lost immediately in the wind, the functionality of fear where any reduction of weight speeds flight, but to no avail. The peregrine inverts, the talons snatch upward, making a shuddering denouement as momentum is seized and forward flight ceases. Only this time the curlew falls to land and the peregrine does not let go. Death comes on a small sandy mound amongst the sea couch-grass, the peregrine transferring its right talon from the breast to the curlew's throat. The arching bill gapes, the flapping wings grow feeble, the lustrous iris wanes, and even before the dark angel settles, the peregrine has lowered its head and is tossing feathers to the interminable wind, the plume the final time they will fly, a transitory monument in final remembrance. The remaining curlews land on the shore only feet from the feasting falcon, and with all threat dispelled now sleep on one leg, bills beneath wings.

The peregrine feeds ravenously, tearing bloodied flesh from the inverted keel, enduring the scouring sand flung from the windward slope of the hummock. Its immense energetic gamble has paid dividends this time, providing enough food to fuel it for several days. It will not always be so. One day such a gamble will fail … and then it shall gamble no more. But for now, life on the edge continues. With the weight of the curlew's carcass lightened by the consumed pectorals, the peregrine drags its kill from the summit of the sandy mound to the shelter of a hollow amongst the grass and, sated, sleeps.

Snow, deep snow, and bitter cold. Under the sickly, flint-coloured sky everything lies still, snow-still. Millions of unique hexagons are lost in a single blanket of white. No wind, no sound, no movement; just the squeak of fresh snow underfoot. The frozen silence is as hard and sharp as obsidian. It almost hurts. A couple of sunspots drift on the horizon. A magpie adorns a field gate like a high-contrast ornament; life imitating the art of Monet's painting. Woodpigeons act as snowploughs, pushing their beaks into the powdery mass flipping it to either side with alternate flicks of the head, enabling them to feed on the cold grass below. A lament of lapwings billows from a field, rippling through the air like a sheet of silk caught in a breeze. The north-east wind has brought a blizzard of winter thrushes and finches to the fields – redwings with gaudy russet flanks and stylish white supercilia; fieldfares with colour-coordinated heads and tails, and bramblings sporting orange breasts and ermine rumps – chic fashion from Scandinavian sophisticates. A male bullfinch kindles from the top of a hawthorn, flaring crimson as it rises in the wan light, and undulates away, white rump blinking; a rare bird out here on the end of the peninsula. A redshank's call rings in the air, the only liquid in this frozen landscape.

Out beyond the reeds which long ago shook themselves free from the shackles of the snow, shelduck have almost vanished from the bay. Curlew are scarce. Only the snowdrifts of dunlin remain in high numbers. As the tide ebbs, small ribbons of redshank drift out and drape themselves across the life-giving mud, their calls glistening in the air like frost on the ground. A small group of knot are clumped around a small pool. A grey plover stands atop a ridge of mud, forlorn and naked in its solitariness. On the river, shrinking with the ebbing tide, a female red-breasted merganser floats, another waif of the weather. It is a stylish duck, set low in the water, with finely vermiculated grey upperparts, a chestnut-brown head and neck, and a long slender vermilion bill, yet its spiky crest has the look of a comic-book electric shock.

Evening is in mid-afternoon. A barn owl unfurls across the darkening fields bathed in its own aura, that inimitable inner glow. From deep within its heart-shaped face, it views the snowy scenery with ebony eyes that absorb the last of the day's light but impart nothing in return. The finery of its plumage resembles a priest's Easter vestments: white and gold with lilac-grey spangles. It strokes the air with muffled wings as if respecting the sanctity of the surrounding silence, and drifts gently, disappearing into the soft folds of dusk's shadows, leaving a diffuse luminescent trail through the mind. As the sun passes below the hanging cloud it catches a passing flock of starlings, polishing them deep burnished red like a fistful of garnets flung in the sky. Ever lower, it ignites the crests of the mud in flaring orange separated by the black of the furrows that converge with perspective towards the distant sea like a grill of lava fissures, then dips below more cloud, hugging the horizon and the shadows return like the crust forming on the surface of cooling magma. Tonight it will be bitterly cold; many creatures will not greet the morning.

Fields are hard and uneven underfoot, white with hoar. Bushes and brambles are rimed with jagged frost. The sky is a fragile blue brushed far above with the curving exhalations of angels. Redshank wisp from river to seashore. The soft rush of their wings whispers as they pass low overhead; strangely intimate, a sound of closeness like the purring of a cat, yet brief, as if such a tender moment of communion is to be feared, rejected and dismissed into the banal indifference of silence. Lapwings call. Their plaintive squeals pierce that icy silence, echoing off the angular air. As the birds feed amongst coronas of prismatic dewdrops, their wing coverts shine violet like luminous epaulettes. Overhead, a single fieldfare stutters its dry rattle, white underwings gleaming in flight. As the sun climbs, the brambles begin to emerge from their pale sheath, darkening and shining like a snake sloughing its old dull skin. In a thawing patch, greening in the intangible warmth, a song thrush melds with the shadows while it forages in the softening ground.

On the coast, there are just memories of the tide, a glistening wet sheen on the mud and a damp strandline. The edge of substance drifts in the shimmering haze of distance. Hunger sated by a woodpigeon taken over the fields by the river yesterday evening, a peregrine is flying for fun in the diamante light of the winter's morning. The freezing air is smooth and crisp and dry: there is no thermic turbulence to contend with today, but no thermals either on which to soar. Curlews blow around it in the wind but it pays them no heed for it has no need to hunt. It climbs through the crisp air, wings feathering the air, enjoying its sensual fluidity all around; the tightness and firmness that must make flight a pleasure – the difference between running on a firm wet beach rather than in the sapping softness of dry sand – small inputs resulting in instant responses. It rises rapidly, heading inland, flight fluid and nonchalant, becoming smaller and smaller, leaving behind just the sound of Sunday church bells drifting across the river calling the faithful to prayer.

Far below, a smaller incarnation perches on a gnarled, lichen-covered post at the edge of the reedbed: a female merlin. She glows bronze in the bright sunlight. She preens her chestnut and cream breast feathers, nibbling them gently between the hooked mandibles of her black-tipped, grey bill. A small feather drifts down to float on the water below like a coracle. She pauses, casting her gaze across the foreshore. Her head bobs occasionally, an outward manifestation of the seething incandescence within. She stills, her attention focused totally on some distant interest. Then back to preening, now her barred tail. She raises her head, shining jet eyes fierce and fathomless, and tenses again; then erupts into the supportive air, the true embodiment of her spirit, flickering low across the tattered stems of marram grass on the low ridge of sand, making a lazy pass at a skylark that has flushed in fright, before alighting once more on a drift log at the edge of the shore. Then away again, straight out towards the far distant sea, flowing over the shining mud, hugging its corrugated surface, direct and very fast. Dunlin rise as one, flashing like a shoal of sardines as they twist, tightening, into the sky. The merlin sweeps into the flock to be absorbed by its cytoplasm, ingested like a food particle into a paramecium, obscured yet still plainly visible, then suddenly ejected from the other side as the dunlin veer seaward and she backs towards land to seek a meal elsewhere.

A front has brought warm air that has chased the snow into the deepest recesses of the shadows, but the ground remains cold. The resulting fog has dissolved the day, the details of the land still swaddled at midday in an intimate cocoon, the edges fuzzy like torchlight in darkness or faith through a glass darkly. So wildlife is come across as if by surprise – a buzzard on a fence post that displays its anxiety by leaning forward to emit a white snake of waste before taking wing to fly just a single post away; a robin trickling its glassy rivulet of sub-song softly over the brambles that drops deeper away into their cover; a weasel standing on its hindlegs on the track that bolts beneath the bushes; a blackbird, shiny from the wet grass in which it is feeding, that panics away, half-hopping half-flying, scolding in alarm; a moorhen that rushes frantically with flailing wings from open grass to the dense reeds of a rhyne – away, always away, from the ever-present toxicity of humanity that has come too close upon them. The scent of death pervades our shape and sound. It is perhaps the saddest thing for those who love wildlife that such love is almost always unrequited; that wish to be closer, to see and to observe is never reciprocated, our interactions are mostly fleeting. Perhaps it is this that makes tameness, when it occurs, so endearing and memorable. From somewhere in the greyness, the aching haunting of a curlew's call trembles the silence, ascending, quavering, enlarging the sky like the dawn light.

By mid-afternoon, the fog has risen into low cloud. Over the mud lifted by the ebbing tide, dunlin vapour shimmers, a glittering silver tracery engraving intricate patterns against the granite-grey sediment and sky, evanescent on the wind. Ten thousand mud-dancers swirl ebullient in a sweeping mud ballet. They stretch and fold, surging across the cloud, pulsing like a protozoan, drifting like a ciliate, protean patterns taking the form of larger animals – a flying dove, a manatee, a swimming plesiosaur, a manta ray – like free-flowing protoplasm. Schizophrenic, part of the mass pretends to land along the water's edge only to be torn skywards again by the centripetal force of the beating heart of the flock which billows like warm breath in cold air, expanding across the sky like a voice thrown heavenwards only to contract again as a returning echo, morphing into swirling tentacles that wrap themselves around each other, spiralling upward then diving again like writhing mating serpents in some ecstatic union. They surge and eddy like flakes in a desktop snow-globe, then settle on the mud like children being called from the playground to their desks, the landing bringing order from the tumult above, the birds still, and all facing into wind. Close by, grey plovers stand sedate, grey-cowled monks moving forward with thoughtful deliberation, bowing slowly as if genuflecting reverently. Then the dunlin are airborne, the snow-globe shaken once more. White flashes pulse rapidly along the line of the flock as thousands of birds sequentially roll left then right in tight choreography, repeatedly turning their gleaming white underparts for brief moments as if a spotlight is being played rapidly from the front to back along the multitude. The repeating patterns cease, a change in colour at the rear of the flock presages a schism as the white undersides turn sharply towards the river and the dark upper sides continue seaward, the flock parting like dividing chromosomes.

Evening near the point, and a ringtail hen harrier hunts low over the reedbed. It seems curiously weightless, a deftness of touch to its flapping, a fragility to its tilting glides, as if the wind might blow it away like a piece of litter. With its wings held in a shallow 'V' over its back, it rocks gently like a funambulist's balancing pole. Its soft shallow wingbeats are full of musical movement, yet laced with menace. It is slim-bodied but lanky in wings and tail, brown with dark streaks, barred boldly on underwings and tail. Its white rump occasionally glints like a beacon. It flies into wind head-down, searching, falling on long glides, rising while flapping. Occasionally, it snaps backwards, jack-knifing in response to the presence of a small bird or mammal, then resumes its course. It curves its wings in a shallow arc, corralling the breeze beneath them to provide momentary stationary lift, as it gives greater scrutiny to the ground below, tail fanned wide and twisting hard to hold position. Four teal burst vertically from a pool nearby, and it turns nimbly, wings accelerating in a flurry to prevent a stall – but the decision to pursue is just too slow, the teal just too far away, and the moment just passed. It returns to its light skimming flight through the gathering darkness, the golden medallions of its eyes now apparent as it lifts its head and passes over the floodbank and out along the coastal reeds, there to drop to roost, sequestered into its cloister.

Five minutes at dusk gives the day its ration of sunshine as the sun drops from beneath the heavy grey shawl into a cleft on the horizon. But such a five minutes! Gorgeous intense melting light, the rays flooding a land starved of direct sun for days, illuminating it with vibrancy, throwing long black shadows, bathing it with a resinous glow, a landscape viewed through amber – the willows deep ochre, the hawthorns dark purple, the reeds warm tawny, the fields luminescent green. The eyes are warmed but the skin is left untouched. It is a light common to the peninsula, a light rich and vivid, mature and warming like whisky, vivacious as a smile, a result of the boundless skies and the flat land and the lack of trees and the presence of the sea that reflects it upward, distilling and refining it. It is the light of home.

A curlew's call quavers through the aqueous grey of the winter solstice. The north-east wind is light but raw, having brought snow flurries overnight, the last vestiges lingering in shelter. Heavy drizzle falls with ambitions of sleet. Brightness glares from a small gap riven between the distant hills and the thick steel banks of cloud welded onto a horizon beyond reach. It points like a cadaverous finger thrust through a hole in a glove. Loose lines of lapwings undulate over the flaccid river, painting the sky with soft wingbeats, brushing the watercolour clouds with their floppy moth-like flight, their wistful calls marrying with the drizzle, their fluid buoyancy so different from the faster thrusting wingbeats and compact formations of their golden plover consorts and that of the lower flocks of angular redshanks moving rapidly over the water. The lost souls of woodpigeons perch forlornly in trees, decorating them as lifelessly as Christmas lights switched off during daylight. A buzzard, sleeked dark by the wet, sits hunched and dejected on a fence post, sated by earthworms or carrion rabbit, its gaze listless and unfocused, waiting for a day with sunshine and thermals on which it can rise clear of this cursed earth and feel the air flow through its feathers once more at height. But for now, all it can do is wait. A grey, damp, bone-chilling day, flat, boring, mind-numbingly dull, another day to be climbed through, survived. A mundane day like so many that form the infrastructure of winter, forgotten but still the framework on which the memories are hung. No longer the frosty, blue-skied snowscapes of our grandparents' reminiscences perpetuated through idealised chocolate-box nostalgia, but altogether a drearier reality. As afternoon folds and the gloom deepens, bushes swell like bruises on an increasingly intimate horizon. The land floats in a dank miasma. The unremitting rain leaches warmth from skin, injecting it with piercing pain. Somewhere overhead in the formless greyness, gulls are heading out to roost, their presence perceptible only from their keening echoing into the blankness of the darkening air.

The light wind is cutting. The eastern horizon subsides like a lower eyelid lazily opening, revealing the brilliant orange cornea of the sun. Six swans beat slowly and heavily along the steaming river, self-immolating in the solar flare like a holy offering. Gradually the sun pulls clear of the church tower, like an airship rising slowly from its mooring mast. The waters burn. There are no low-level clouds today: the frigid air holds no water vapour, resulting in that liquid clarity of light peculiar to a day ahead of coming snow; far horizons close; field boundaries visible at the edge of the moor ten miles distant, already dusted lightly white. Duck are in flight. Teal are fast and frantic, light and skittish as if not quite in control. Wigeon are heavier, more stable and direct, less neurotic. When they land, the teal remain tense and jittery, heads and bills raised, tails cocked, fuelled by angst, febrile, on the edge of flight again; the wigeon more composed and impassive. Along the coast, the wind carries the noise of the restless rolling of the high spring tide. Skylarks, displaced from the front of the frosted saltmarsh grass by the seawater, chirrup with anxiety overhead their drowned haunts as they mix incongruously with passing herring gulls.

Slack water brings cessation to the gulls' feeding. They come together to form close-knit flocks high on the marsh or swimming on the river. A female peregrine, patinaed like steel in the low rays of the winter sun, her body hard and taut, sweeps across the marsh playfully harassing a carrion crow that is unappreciative of the reversal of its own bullying tactics. The crows have been hard pressed this morning, harried mercilessly by gulls as they carried voles, drowned by the flooding tide, to drier land to feed. The peregrine glides out along the edge of the river and comes to rest on a shingle ridge, her horizontal stance, stocky, squat, and malevolent as she searches for a new hunting route. She sallies out once more, skimming low over the marsh in a wide arc, but returns to the same perch. Having failed to flush anything, she adopts an upright, less-threatening pose, and proceeds to preen herself. Behind her the dredger throbs by, riding high, its orange lower hull clear of the water, its passage marking the beginning of the ebb tide, yet its crew as oblivious to the peregrine as the falcon is to them – worlds apart.

Frost hides in the late morning shadows, but out in the fields the molehills are drying in the weak sun, sandy archipelagos in a Pacific of green. Many have collapsed like calderas where the rabbits have burrowed down from the top. Yet the earth is moving from one, the seismic activity of a mole causing the nearest hill to erupt with fresh dark soil. Next to it a male blackbird feeds in the sunlit dampness of the pasture. It is a first-year bird, its brown primaries retained from its juvenile plumage like a mismatched car body repair awaiting a respray, full blackness to be achieved only through next autumn's moult. It cocks its head to one side, seeking movement before jabbing its yellow bill earthward to snatch a pink wriggling earthworm or a shiny black beetle. It has selected this place with care, for the tremors are causing the invertebrates to move towards the surface where they make easy pickings for the hungry thrush.

Morning breaks white under deep violet-grey clouds as the snowstorm departs to the north, its edges blurred like a still-wet watercolour. The days of frost before last night's snow have left the freshwater lagoon completely frozen, the ice coloured a strange flat yellow-green. Now the only open water is on the river and the sea itself. Most birds have been forced to leave; overhead that movement continues as small flocks of fieldfares flee westwards with the wind behind them, the conditions too harsh for even these hardy souls. The saltmarsh is empty, the snow, skinny and lean, stripped from its flat surface by the incessant wind. Snow makes the wind visible; the crisp channels where it blows and scours, the soft and voluptuous drifts where it eddies in sheltered gullies. Only the narrow dark brown line between the white shore and the grey sea, ever widening as the tide ebbs, holds life; a relative frenzy in the still landscape as a few waders run and forage and fly. The muddy sea breaks over an ice cliff along the shore, depositing fine sediment on the snow and breaking small chunks off into icebergs; a scene more reminiscent of the Arctic than western England. A common gull, belied by its name for it is uncommon here, flares to land on the desolate shore just beyond the reach of the waves, its white underwings, tipped black, held high above its head in angelic pose before it hunches down into the cold. Where the reeds have been flattened, snow has settled. Where they still stand, it has been sifted and deflected leaving the reeds tawny. Fence posts are capped white. Sheep huddle in the lee of a hedge, their yellowed fleeces encrusted with pristine snow as they nibble a few exposed stems of withered grass. Three snipe, displaced from the frozen marshes, flush from an icy ditch and pitch into the adjacent pallid field seeking somewhere with no resistance to their probing bills.

Along the coast path, a headless redshank lies on its back, its rib cage naked, its unplucked wings part-open, curved around it, the flight feathers rising out of the snow like Neolithic standing stones encircling the altar of its sternum; the kill absurdly mimicking a place of sacrifice within itself. Close to are the remains of another kill, a golden plover, but this is just a black leg, a yellowed pelvis, and a tuft of golden-spangled feathers from beneath what had been a tail, the leg grotesquely pointing at the sky as if giving a clue as to where its killer came from. There are five corpses along the coast path in total, all stripped and devoured, neat piles of feathers marking their final resting places; strange when months go by without the presence of a single one. Does the snow make the birds more vulnerable to the hawks and, in times of hardship for most species, do the hawks have a glut? Or has the scarcity of land birds driven the raptors to concentrate along the shore? Perhaps; yet none is apparent this day. Maybe the remains of prey are simply more conspicuous in snow. One body, seemingly that of a dunlin, displays chewed feather shafts, a sign that a fox has eaten here, but whether it has caught an individual enfeebled by cold while hunting on the mudflats or scavenged the carcass of a hawk's kill, the bird's remains give no clue.

It is said to be pretty, this snow; robed in beauty, bright and full of wonder. And when the sun shines on it, it is. But when the grey clouds hang low and the light dulls, the landscapes become hard and bleak and flinty. Then only the faded ochre of the reeds fringing the coast and rhynes provide sanctuary to the eye from the monochrome of burnt umber trees and bushes and tarnished white snow. There is little beauty then; just an altogether more sordid reality, for everywhere there is the pain of cold; always the pain of cold, unrelenting and exacerbated by the pitiless easterly wind sucking away body heat, leaving only numbness.

Does any other killer tread behind a mask so fair?
Beguiling and with beauty yet it stalks without a care,
It saps away at body heat gives nothing in return
But an icy grave for many for pity it does spurn

It comes with joy and wonder, provokes laughter and delight
And leaches colour from the sky as fields turn sparkling white
Yet when the sun is over and the stars twinkle at night
Its frigid blade unsheathes to kill without malice or spite

It adorns a million calendars and countless Christmas cards
Deceptive white, its innocence conceals its icy shards
Yet few spare thoughts for the lives it takes and wantonly discards
All we see is the prettiness and the rest we disregard.

JANUARY
WINGS OF SUPPLICATION

And dawn was the first dawn and light was the first light; ancient and mystifying – layers of ivory mist smoking from a flat grey horizonless sea, lapping at the edge of the mud, lapping at the very edge of the world, shards of waders' calls crystallising in the frigid air, yet trembling and softened by the airborne dew like the constant tinkling of distant treble wind chimes; the music of comfort and fear. In its boundless transcendence, squat and cerise, an amoeba morphs slowly from the lightening void, crawling upwards against the gravity that would deny it, reddening with the exertion of pulling itself into a perfect circle, the birth pangs of the day. Inexorably it rises along its arc, a scarlet disc following a primordial urge, irresistibly upwards, yellowing, dissolving, whitening, until surpassing all shape it diffuses into boundless light, at one with the mist.

An hour later and New Year comes with magic – a land rimed by hoar frost sparkling in the bright winter sun, straggly brambles transformed into diamond tiaras, potholes glazed with glinting glass. Above it all, a vast sapphire sky, clear and limitless, no points of reference, just dazzling transparency pervading the sea and river and pools below. Nine wigeon nuzzle amongst the rippling wavelets in the transient convoluted bays formed by the tide, the males' heads of burnished copper with gleaming topaz forecrowns glowing in the rich light, whistles lost to the distance. Along the edge of the river, avocets, delicate of form and movement but bold of plumage, step serenely in the shallows on ice-blue legs, scything the water with recurved bills, their sublime curves granting beguiling grace, an elegance of elongation, pied paragons; exquisite avian fashionistas. When they fly, the sunlight laces through their translucent wings so that even at a distance they seem delicate and fragile, like crystal lit from within. A heron, hunkered down in the shadow of the sluice, retracts its head even further between its shoulders, meditating on patience.

Overhead, revelling in the clarity of the cold, a male peregrine drifts across the flawless sky from the river to the sea, then west along the coast, seeking out the wader roosts on this high spring tide. He spirals tightly, climbing into the void, cavorting in the sun-filled stillness, revelling in the ecstasy of flight, watched by unseen thousands of eyes below. The stoop when it comes has no forewarning: the falcon simply stops flying as if he has been shot, falling vertically, wings closed, primaries barely extended to provide directional stability, tail sleeked, an ebony arrowhead fuelled by gravity streaking earthward. At two hundred feet he trims his wings and the vertical descent becomes a sweeping shallowing curve. The high tide roost of waders flares like a struck match, panic surging from the vortex of the heaving flock, all rational thought destroyed, all cognitive behaviour lost to the lancing flood of adrenalin sweeping aside everything, the randomness of fleeing now total, the chances of surviving in a flock high until the statistics run out. At fifty feet the peregrine flails the flocks and a knot dies from the impact with gravitational velocity. Now burdened with prey, the falcon labours inland across the lagoons and saltmarsh, coming to rest in the grass below a favoured drift log. Altering his stance and the disposition of his prey, he commences to pluck. A plume of feathers billows from the corpse, its silent coronach, tousled by the light breeze. A female materialises on the log above him, bobbing with excitement and wittering piercing screams of petulance. She jumps down alongside her smaller mate and when he remains reticent to share, accosts him to supplant his place at the meal. But she is rebuffed with mantled wings and open bill and vehement shrieks: in winter, hunger triumphs over altruism. The female remains, standing to one side, for the knot is large enough that pickings may remain even after the male has stripped the steaming deep maroon pectorals from the gleaming ivory of the jutting sternum.

Even with the midday sun past its zenith, frost remains folded into shady hollows. To the west, snow clings to the high moors. Along the wind-wracked shoreline, the cord-grass glows golden in the early afternoon sun. Seaward of the fringing reedbed, two female roe deer feed in the sodden marsh, their large soft ears twisting back and forth trying to filter danger from the soughing sea. Alarmed, they run, stotting like antelopes, fanning their white rump hair, flashing the danger to distantly remembered herds. The sodden marsh spits snipe into the air. They rasp like tearing Velcro as they rip themselves from the ground, zigzagging low across the grass before towering away into the sky with grating calls, skying away over the reeds. Immediately, two jack snipe follow, ejecting violently but silently from underfoot. Short and squat, they jink only briefly before dropping weakly back into cover. A water rail, narrow-bodied and long-necked, propels itself from the edge of a stagnant pool, rancid with sweet decay, seasoned by saltiness, and littered with storm-driven flotsam and jetsam. Legs trailing, it snatches for the safety of the reeds, tumbling hurriedly from sight. Trapped in these pools is the detritus from distant lands – a punctured football, a faded Lucozade bottle, a broken camera strap, a shiny deflated party balloon, a roll-on deodorant container, a bright blue moulded plastic stool, and an ancient rusted oil drum that has been tossed around by the tide and has flattened the reeds like some kind of perverse harvester. The swampy mud sucks at boots, releasing noxious smells to the cold wind that quickly dilutes them to nothingness. In the cord-grass lies the mangled body of a curlew, its eye sockets hollow and its curved bill twisted through an unnatural angle. It is mud-spattered and encrusted with sand, but whether it simply died or is the remains of a kill is impossible to tell. Nearby, the skeleton of a shore crab lies upside down on the sand, claws clutching insanely at the sky. Beyond that, the bleached ribcage of a colossal ancient dragon lies with its back to the shore, its ribs extending longingly towards the land of its ancestors far over the sea, and just as mythically, for with a subtle shift in the light they are reduced to the glistening rivulets of low tide in the long parallel runnels of the mud. The mud disappears to the horizon. It is split by the line of light that moves as the viewer walks. Ahead, away from the sun, it is pale and milky but behind that line, into the sun, it becomes dark like molasses. A place is all about perspective; it changes with viewpoint, it changes with time; in an hour the light will have shifted, the tide will have risen or ebbed – the place is still the same yet it will be different. Far out over the flats, the shadows of small billowing clouds look like shell holes in the mud with accompanying puffs of smoke above. In the silence, beyond all, a thousand dunlin equivocate, up and down, brown and white, back and forth, before drifting down to the surface, like sleet disappearing on landing.

Atop a fence post ferments a female merlin, effervescent, too much energy for her frame to contain, a bird forged in a furnace whose heat has never cooled, ever on the edge of flight, head bobbing agitatedly, scanning back and forth before turning backwards over her mantle, staring intently with dark bottomless eyes. And then she is away, flickering fast and low, threshing the lapwings from the starlings as they plume into the sky. She ignores them all, intent focused on a patch of meadow ahead, ordinary until a meadow pipit discharges from it, the last act of its life – a life that leaves its physical form in a puff of feather dust momentarily suspended beside it then lost to the wind and its executioner's wingbeats. The merlin barely breaks rhythm, the merest syncopation, as she thrusts out her left leg to snatch the flaccid body away from its life force, and carries it drooping and heavy to a favoured perch on a low branch of a small dead tree. Immediately she begins to pluck, one yellow foot clamping the soft body to the branch, its head hanging limp beneath, beak open, a single drip of blood forming at its tip. She rips the spotted feathers from the breast, tossing them into the breeze and wiping those clagging her bill on the bark before finally the consummative moment when her hooked bill tears the hot bloodied flesh below and she feeds.

The storm's winds have backed from south-west to north, funnelling Arctic cold across the country, and then departed in gusts like the last convulsions of a dying animal. The temperature has plummeted. The sea is flat sheet pewter. Cloud glowers. Sleet falls softly from an opaque white sky. Wet reeds glow golden with an inner light; leaves are heavy and still now the wind has gone. Gulls stream in their hundreds along the brimming river. Teal dabble silently close in amongst the small tidal pools along the riverbank. The cream triangular patch below the males' tails and white horizontal lines along their flanks flash in the cold gloom like reflective strips on safety clothing. Further out, at the edge of the open water, wigeon whistle wistfully into the first wisps of the evening mist. A pair of mallards dabble beneath a bank of a lagoon with six little grebes bobbing around them, like two oil tankers and their attendant tugboats. Darkness skitters from the lengthening shadows as the sun dips below the western hills. The light is leaving. Air thickens with cold. With wings of supplication raised above it, an apparition drifts over a hedge, tilting back and forth, wafting over the field, praying for voles or release from purgatory. It wheels without wingbeats, its black pinions playing the air, conjuring lift where there should be none, and makes another pass across the grass – an apparition that the mind wills to remain but, rising over another hedge and manifesting itself transiently as a male hen harrier, becomes nebulous again in the rising mist. As night falls, the sleet becomes snow and starts to settle.

Hushed. Snow silent. Only the Siberian wind skims over the pastures, singing its tired songs through the blasted bushes. The land is white under violet-grey skies, the snow on the ground scoured and furrowed by the biting wind, the trees and bushes stark and black, the landscape unfamiliar. The eye is parched of colour; the soul is parched of vitality, the cold leaching it from the body, sucking heat from the extremities, the warmth an osmotic flow from the skin, a haemorrhage impossible to staunch. The rolling flocks of starlings are becalmed. The strong wind has beaten them into the lee of stunted hedges. Lapwings are huddled into the flatness of a field, trying to shelter behind tufts of grass. The blackness of their mantles, part-covered by the drifting flakes, resembles the range of nearby molehills. The archipelago, volcanic against the white ocean around them, indicates that while it may be freezing above ground the moles remain active below. A snipe lands in a field and hurries towards the cover of longer grass, its gait inebriated and ungainly as it struggles through the snow on short legs, its outsize bill catching occasionally in the drifts, capsizing it.

Along the coast path, light snow falls horizontally; not continental dry powder snow but maritime wet snow that packs tight and scrunches underfoot. The sea churns brown. Birds are barely surviving. A robin perches weakly on a snow-doused bramble – the archetypal Christmas card, its prettiness tempered by the knowledge that this is probably its last day alive. A woodcock bursts from the base of a stile, a mosaic of gingers and chestnut browns, a little piece of woodland floor as out of place amongst the anaemic grasses and coastal reeds as a clown cast in a Shakespearean tragedy that it brings forth a physical gasp of surprise; an interloper ripped silently by frost from its sylvan glades to seek softer ground on the coast. Snipe-like but heavier, it arches away from underfoot, pulling heavily into the air on rounded pumping wings, then lurches drunkenly to the left, crashing down into the reeds, disappearing between the stems and a bank of snow, enfeebled by cold and hunger. A bedraggled woodpigeon, its belly feathers sullied by snow and mud, pecks apathetically at the leaflets of an ice-glazed sea radish, its pale iris dulled and vacant, its lifeblood draining with the effort of surviving. Only a lone common gull seams at ease, flapping low overhead, its plumage a perfect rendering of the landscape below. A redshank calls, a fragile glint of sound in the frigid air, unstable, hanging like a drop of water the moment before it falls from the tip of an icicle.

There is no wader roost today, no time for standing sleeping. On the mud a thick crust of ice marks the limit of last night's high tide, a low wall of sharp, jagged, mud-doused cliffs in contrast to the smooth contours of the clean white snow. In the lee of these, small groups of redshank and turnstone huddle tightly together. On the edge of one group, a purple sandpiper pecks disconsolately at the mud. Normally a denizen of the rocky shore, today it is just another displaced bird. A gaunt buzzard stands sentinel on a bleached drift-branch on the foreshore, forced from its fields to find food in alien surroundings. It flaps heavily to get airborne, then glides on broad wings, low along the foreshore smoking waders from their shelter. Later it returns, continuing to make short apathetic passes at the waders as if trying to learn their responses. But their tight jinking flight remains too quick for a bird whose main food is carrion and rabbits. The buzzard rests: the waders feed. Three great black-backed gulls approach low along the shore. Their wing-beats are deep and ponderous yet curiously buoyant. Their guttural calls are resonant, each hanging in the wind after the next has begun, like an echo. The gulls spot the buzzard atop its post and change course, spiralling in around it, curious rather than vindictive. Yet the buzzard is spooked by their unfamiliarity; these are not the usual crows it knows. It launches into the air flipping sharply onto its back, throwing beak and talons upwards, grappling into the empty air in wilful defence of the threat it perceives from these three birds that dwarf it. The gulls circle it one more time but the buzzard is free and flies strongly away down the shore, away from this strange land of terrors.

Beneath a hedgerow an immature greenfinch lies dead, a lifeless corpse perfect in form but lacking substance, the exigencies of negative energy equations coalescing in the brute reality of starvation. The core tenet of evolutionary theory or the fickleness of chance? The insatiable cold has stripped away its warmth and life, leaving its eyes concave and dull. Its feathers are now held only loosely in place by desiccated skin and bone. The wind has tunnelled beneath the yellow-brown breast, ruffling grey down to the surface, and begun to pluck it free. Strange, is it not, that there is no chemical difference between the living and the dead, no change in the physical entity? Yet that spark that confers life has gone, that spark that has been handed like a relay baton from generation to generation, from life form to life form unbroken through millions of years; the still unknown something that rides a knife-edge between being and not being, has in this instance ended in the quiet solitude beneath this hawthorn bush at this time, like an ocean wave faltering at its zenith on a sandy beach. This tiny dead bird, not even having had a chance to breed: its spark has simply been discarded and become part of the chaff of evolution.

A fragile dawn breaks bitter and silent, a simple journey through the greyscale. Light remains crepuscular beneath thick banks of congealed cloud. To the south-east, a ragged fracture the colour of raw albumen is the only discernible sign that the sun has risen. The northerly wind remains – freezing and blustery and pitiless. It has skimmed the surface, erasing footprints, drifting the snow into the lee of banks and hedges. The prettiness of winter has been lost. Bleak has replaced picturesque. Colour has gone, the impoverished palette monochrome infused with sepia. Trees and hedges stand stark and skeletal above fields of frozen snow, twisted black branches like emaciated arthritic fingers, their fairy tale coverings lost days ago, ungloved and assaulted by the wind. Those of the ancient gnarled elders fret squeakily, mimicking birds. Only the tangled brambles have held a broken covering of snow. The incessant cold harangues bodies, sucks heat from extremities, claws at the core, demands shivers. Two carrion crows search methodically for food where dead grass emerges from the white surface, two glossy black puffballs, almost spherical, curiously and arrestingly attractive, pacing about like black-cloaked undertakers. Fieldfares drip steadily eastward towards the point, mostly silent, too little energy to spare except for an occasional harsh chatter. A peregrine flickers through the last dregs of darkness and shakes a sheet of lapwings from the fields. They levitate as one, loosely flapping and fluid, flashing in the wind, their pied wings riveting the attention like Aldis lamps blinking encrypted Morse messages from the sky.

The sea has gone; the mudflats have risen and pushed it away into some unwanted corner. In the wan morning sun, partially liberated by a gap in the cloud, glittering white ribbons of birds ripple over its dark ribbed surface, a photographic negative of the white land with its dark birds. The distance steals their identity; ambiguity between gull or shelduck. The frozen lagoons are lifeless; their edges iced from previous days and now white under a dusting of snow, the dark and opaque centres, frozen only last night, bearing the petrified patterns of the wind and tidal ingress. Out on the saltmarsh the wing of a dead swan flaps pathetically in the gusts as if some force from the afterlife is entreating it to fly again. But nothing flies save a few herring gulls hanging loosely on the wind, seemingly oblivious to the cold. Snow-reflected light ripples along their undersides in place of the usual shadows bestowing them an ethereal quality. They glow exquisitely white against the dark grey sky, the tips of their wings sharply black, their bills crisp yellow and red. The forlorn whistles of wigeon drift over the empty tidal creeks as they feed on the grass and algae along the top of the riverbank. In the fields, lapwings fold themselves once more into their forms, huddling down to shelter amongst the tussocks. In the lee of a ruined wall, a wren flits through the withered brown deformities that once were thistles. A song thrush picks at the shrivelled remnants of berries on the hawthorn bushes, trying to extract some last shred of nourishment. All is silent; only the wind whistles its spiteful tune. An unseen blackbird suddenly scolds concern from the cadaverous form of a hedge, haggard and petrified, like the ancient relic of something once lush with vitality. It does not fly. Flight means immediate loss of heat and diminished chances of survival. From the shadow of thickening cloud, falling ice crystals twinkle only to become lost on the snowy ground.

Morning is the colour of cold; cowled and sullen under the bitter icing of winter. The piercing wind has abated; a clammy mist now tight upon the land. Light is heavy. A morning without horizons; distance and perspective lost concepts. Just the cold, seeping insidiously, sapping the vitality of warmth and energy from bodies: a day for surviving. The recent freezing rain has drilled holes in the thawing snow like shipworm in timber. Pastel pigment is squeezing back into a landscape parched of colour for days. The remaining snow lies in narrow strips along field edges like fungus on rotting wood. Lapwings flop listlessly into the air, leaving their wistful calls behind them. Along the lane someone has placed a lost glove on a fencepost, its well-worn fingers splayed, like some medieval warning: 'Go no further: Plague'. A goldcrest forages along a hedgerow, a transitory presence moving like a wisp, allowing mere glimpses of itself, already gone before eyes can clearly focus upon it, deep in the shifting shadows of the bramble shrouds. Nearby, a buzzard ceases walking, stopping to pick a heavy earthworm from the wet muddy surface; a common food source for it in winter. It launches itself into the air, skimming inches above the grass on broad outstretched wings and, with a couple of powerful flaps, alights on a nearby fencepost, its faint shadow skating up to greet it lightly as it lands. With small mammals inactive, a female kestrel is hunting birds. In the guise of a sparrowhawk she shimmers low over the pallid fields and jumps a hedge to surprise the far side, but she is learning and her technique is still clumsy. Failing to catch anything, she disappears along the bushes to try again.

By late afternoon the mist has lifted to reveal another layer of sombre blankness. Low stratus hugs the land, featureless like a divine ice rink, the full flood tide rising to meet it only fractionally darker. In the narrow space between cloud and sea, just above the lapping waves, straggling lines of curlew and squadrons of shelduck, one escorted by a cormorant, head towards the point. Sleet is falling softly from the sky. Distantly, in the greyness, darker grey, like smoke roiling gently on the breeze, multitudes of dunlin are sifted in diagonal lines, held but for a moment, then curving into sinuous waves rippling through the gloom, blooming white and recoiling dark, diaphanous pale ribbons weaving interlacing patterns on the imperceptible motions of the ancient rhythms of the air, dancing to a symphony only they can hear, the flock expanding and contracting rhythmically as if the sky itself is breathing. Out on the saltmarsh, forlorn upon a post, feathers damp, darkened and dishevelled, a peregrine waits out the eternity of the afternoon, eyes alert within a cloak of ennui. It crouches forward, transferring its weight from one foot to the other, kneading the rotten post with its talons like the pulsing paw of a pet cat being stroked on a lap. It preens abstractedly, raises its tail high and defecates. Seemingly on the edge of flight, it part-opens its wings and ruffles its plumage, shakes its body rolling it back and forth, becoming angular yet still soft, as if wearing a silver-grey tulle-draped taffeta evening dress. Then it returns to an upright stance and its sempiternal vigil. It will roost here in the open now until the dawn disturbs its slumber and hunger carries it into the skies once more.

Morning limps anaemic from the night sky, the light insipid under malevolent clouds broken by a single shard of clear sky like a tarnished silver stiletto thrust through their heart. The days since the snow thawed have been warmer, but rain has poured almost incessantly as depression has followed depression rolling in off the Atlantic, re-establishing prevailing weather patterns, forcing the cold continental air back to the east. Rain batters diagonally, flung by the ferocious wind into the floods of standing water pooled across the grass. Its surface shudders under the onslaught. The drenched land seems to exude despair over how much more water it can take. Water does not move here: there are no ripples or bubbles, or sounds of gurgling or babbling, for there are no inclines in this flat land at the edge of the sea. Even the river's flow is ambivalent, for it changes its languid direction four times a day. Water simply seeps slowly and imperceptibly and without fuss. But now the rhynes are overflowing, ponds are brimming, tracks are flooded, fields shine. Water lies in shattered panes across the grass like glass blown out of the sky. The moles have migrated to higher ground; the complexes of new spoil tips marking their recent tunnelling have erupted along the old dune line. And still it rains. Birds are sodden. A female kestrel seeks refuge on the windowsill on the lee side of the house, her barred plumage slicked and matted, the bobbing of her head quelled by the wet, the depth of her fear in her deep black eyes diluted by the downpour. She stares with unblinking incomprehension through the glass at her deepest dread seated just a metre away, shakes her feathers with a violent convulsion as if trying to rid herself of some burdensome parasite, and hunches her head into its body, to wait with abject patience.

The drowned fields brighten in the tepid light of the low afternoon sun. A slight shimmer on the surface of the shallow floodwaters betrays the presence of a water rail as it overcomes its agoraphobia and ventures to feed along the base of a hedge. It is full of pent-up nervous energy, fearful anxiety so much a way of life that even a robin alighting nearby sends it scurrying back into cover. It ventures out again, short tail cocked and flicking with apprehension, each step of its long pink toes placed with consideration, its curved red bill picking flotsam precisely from the flood. Yet the outside world is just too wide for such timidity, and it suddenly races into the tall grass, squeezing its laterally-compressed body back into reassuringly narrow spaces. A group of redshanks peck at their reflections in platinum pools, extracting food from the points where their beaks intersect each other through the surface tension.

In the stark branches of a stunted hawthorn, bright with yellow lichen, a wren bobs dementedly. It shouts out its mighty challenge to the world beyond, thrusting itself upwards and forwards on tiptoe, cocked tail twitching frantically, but darts back into the enveloping safety of the brambles at the least sign of nearby movement. A few bushes away, the reason for the wren's neurosis becomes apparent as a female sparrowhawk lands on a fence post, carrying a blackbird. She hunches onto its upturned breast, one foot tightening across its throat. As death overcomes the blackbird, its legs and toes that have grasped so tightly to life and the empty air stretch slowly to their limits in some macabre mockery of orgasmic ecstasy. The sparrowhawk bends to pluck.

Afternoon hunches into evening. The sun is white and glaring, welding the oncoming darkness to the hills. As it dips towards the horizon, warmth deserts the day, radiating upward, leaving the rhynes to steam like some unworldly witch's brew, a white miasma curling from black liquid. With the last colour fading from the land, the western sky glows briefly, a fragile transparent orange and turquoise. A blackbird chinks in the sharpening stillness, stuttering its anxiety into the fading light, a series of hard-edged shiny notes like a teaspoon tapped on a porcelain teacup, a call riven with angst, a quintessential sound of an English winter dusk; it is almost as if the bird is afraid of the coming dark. Chevrons of gulls wing seaward into the faded embers of the sunset to roost on the low-tide mudflats, their wailing laughter echoing off the flat flint sheets of sky and sea, filling the space between.

Suddenly there is a hush to the already hushed air, a presence palpable yet invisible, a luminosity indefinable, a serial bubble of calm in an already windless quietude. Blooming from behind the watcher, a barn owl wafts, rocking gently in the crisp still air, soft and silent, seeming to radiate light around it from some incandescent core that shimmers as softly as its feathers stroke the air. It holds its unblemished angelic wings aloft, as if gaining lift by heavenly means between the lightest of downbeats which caress the air tenderly, coaxing it, encouraging its support; it makes the act of flying surprising intimate and sensual. It floats, and in floating sets free the earthbound shackles of the watcher's soul which lifts in a response to the owl in a way that no other bird can elicit; excitement mixed with awe, envy mixed with marvel. But the dark forces are gathering. Three black-clad zealots that hate hooked beaks and talons with an almost religious fervour converge from disparate angles, hurling their abuse and trying to force the owl to the ground. Yet it is as light-winged and dextrous as the crows are heavy and clumsy; with a flip and some twists it evades their attentions with an ease bordering upon contempt, and with a few deep wingbeats it bounds away from their lumbering pursuit and disappears beyond a hedge. And on the memory the watcher's soul continues to float in perpetuity.

Oh, blaze in the soft-dying evening light
Blaze through the greyness of dusk's gatherings
Blaze in the silence of your lilting flight,
And lift my soul on your Gabriellan wings

Oh, blaze while all around the shadows steal
O'er fading fields, through chill that day's end brings
Oh, blaze now white owl ethereal
For you seem not earthbound as other things

Blaze through soft-dying corners of my mind
Blaze through the patina of passing time,
Your memory shines, bright and unconfined
So blaze now, spread your wings, white owl of mine

95

FEBRUARY
UNABASHED VIVACITY

Lonely is the point, a place raked by biting winter winds, scoured by breaking waves; a blasted surface of sand and stones, pocked with water-filled hollows and broken by miniature cliffs. Fragments of shells fringe the edge where the sea couch-grass starts to grow. Far beyond the very end of the road, this is the very end of land itself, a place of brightness where the light rises into the air from the water all about or shines upwards from the glistening mud left behind by the absent tide. This is land laid down, not land uplifted; gentle land formed by sedimentation, not land spewed molten from volcanic fissures nor hewn by glaciers. Although exposed to the external belligerence of wind and tide, these are ordeals that have been smoothed over and forgotten, leaving none of the internal scars from igneous trauma. It is horizontal land, edge land, fragile land, far distant from the stolidity of central land where tectonic tremors have compressed it and pressured it, raising it into scarps and jagged mountains. The flatness bequeaths its wildness, the big skies and spectacular cloudscapes, the wide expanse of the river and the mudflats, the lack of vertical lines, for nothing breaks the distant blue hills of the horizon and there is no cover here to provide intimacy, nothing to break the wind or absorb the distance of the curlews' liquid calls. When the wind has dropped, or in the sultry warmth of a summer's evening, it is a place of seduction, somewhere to stand and be restful, a place where the stillness allows quiet contemplation, an extraordinary place that sets the soul free, giving it space to soar. But today, after overnight snow, it is desolate, inhabited only by the eternal optimism of a great black-backed gull and disdained by a passing snipe displaced by the hardened marsh. The wind, mean and vicious, metallic with debilitating cold, bores into any gaps in plumage or pelage, hollowing out the heat inside. The waders are absent, far, far out across the mudflats beyond even binocular view, leaving just the shrapnel of the tide wrack and a snowdrift in the lee of a sandbar. Behind the shore, the snow has been too light to form a white blanket and the withered tawny stems stand proud from the white tussocks in a sickly dilute skewbald mottling as if the land is diseased. On the white blaze of a footpath through the reedbed a male reed bunting searches fervently for food, scuffling its fanned wings and tail to extricate itself each time it founders in the snow, sending miniature snowballs skittering across the surface. It opens and closes its beak while it forages as if making silent prayers for food, but with these unanswered it flies up onto one of the dry ochre reed stems rustling in the pernicious wind, and away to try elsewhere.

Behind the reeds, the saltmarsh is empty save a single common gull banking overhead in the wind, a bird of ice-coloured plumage and the curious opaque luminosity of cold as if it is cloned from the snow clouds themselves. Mid-morning, and light flakes still scurry on the spiteful easterly wind. The wan sun is golden, refracted through the clouds; it gilds the pools and the wet mud of the steep riverbanks, reflecting up, glowing against the dark slate sky with the soft patina of a late afternoon: a day in a time warp. On a pool in the lee of a bank swims a waterfowl collection as if assembled by a divine curator – three pairs of shoveler and an unattached female, three pairs of wigeon, two pairs of mallard, and a pair of teal. They are nervous and restive, turning in tight circles with necks stretched upwards on high alert. Yet the half-dozen little grebes with them are unconcerned, diving for food and bobbing back up like pale brown rounded corks, their fluffy rear ends resembling shaving brushes. Finally, unease explodes into flight as the teal cannon into the air and thrust towards the river. The other ducks waver on the edge of leaving, yet something draws them to remain, the bristling anxiety emanating from the neurotic teal now calming like the ripples on the pool from their departure. Overhead, skylarks are in ascension; the sky is full of them, teardrops of sonnets drifting behind like audible snowflakes, the birds lost in a world of white. Gates are dark leeward and white windward, the snow encrusted like spray-on shaving foam. Most fields are deserted. In only one have the stock not been moved to inside shelter; a flock of sheep remain sitting forlornly in the snow. A broken hay bale provides adequate forage and yet all eyes look balefully upon the passer-by as if imploring them for a warm barn.

Lonely is the Point, a blasted fragment
of land, if land it can be called. In torment,
battered by winter winds that never sleep
and bruised by waves that shift its sediment.

Lonely is the Point, place of mud and sand
of desolation, the very end of land
far beyond beyond and the silvered grass
outwith the marsh where light seems to expand.

Lonely is the Point, low land and water
gleaming with bright light that does not falter
shimmering in haze or dancing in the
rain, remaining wild and full of wonder.

Lonely is the Point, where sea meets river
glistening waters that twice deliver
the sweeping flood tides of each day and night
reducing the land to a mere sliver.

Lonely is the Point, scabrous winds bite grey,
and in the wet wan light at break of day
birds play games of life and death as hawk and
waders sway to evade or become prey.

Lonely is the Point, here gulls make laughter
that echoes in the emptiness and after
tide has ebbed and sea retreated, shelduck
rest and preen and flocks of waders gather.

Lonely is the Point, in rain or sun's glare
where magic light plays through aqueous air
and rainbows soar above the sea. A place
that draws one to behold and stand and stare.

A male sparrowhawk comes to rest on a fence post, abrupt in the landscape like an unfinished thought. His glaring sulphurous irides flare manically as they sweep their surroundings, shallow and hard and glassy with a crazed vacant ferocity, a bird seemingly teetering on the brink of insanity. The post holds him physically; the need to be still and to rest are shackles that his body cannot avoid, but his mind still rides the wind. Even then, with his body stationary, his head turns constantly, his eyes plotting the course of his next speed-rush, for motion is sacred to a sparrowhawk, it worships it; it is always moving, the blur in its peripheral vision the opiate it craves. He launches himself from the post, wingbeats furiously polishing the air, and settles into a dashing glide, coursing fast and low across the winter-worn fields, over the torn hedges, skimming past the jaded sheep, along the flooded rhynes, a solid form yet with liquid presence, flowing like molten wax. Twisting his long tail he tilts sharply up and left, pouring over the dormant pleached stems of a hedge, then plunging sharply down, flowing right, disappearing momentarily from view on a parallel trajectory, then spilling back over the bushes, ambushing those birds he had spied ahead. Flushed from the ground, and despite pulsing heart and frantic wingbeats, oblivion streaks from the air and ends the chaffinch's life before it could have been truly aware of the danger. Birds spend their entire lives in fear, never knowing the joy of simple contentment; it is always degraded by the dread of extreme violence and sudden death; the need for eternal watchfulness. Most of humankind long ago lost such fear; it remains subliminal, distant, a fear of something shapeless and undefined, of something perversely to be enjoyed vicariously through thrillers and horror stories or films that caricature it, that can be put away at any time of choosing to return to the normality of a fearless life. Yet for other creatures it pervades their every wakeful moment as well as their sleep.

Frost glitters blue. Beneath a flawless sky, the land lies layered, flat and depthless, distance now an abstract concept. Colour has been sapped away, everything diluted to pastel shades washed with blue. Shelduck float on the darker blue translucence of a gentle swell that steams around them in the cold air. Reflected light plays in ripples along their flanks. A redshank's call pings off the angular shards of the shattered silence, dying from the moment it was ejected from the bird's syrinx, falling away and fading like reflected reflections, until somewhere in the dimness it vanishes, yet echoing still inside the ear long after it has been lost to the cold. The river bleeds like mercury between the fields. The rough pastures are hardened and lumpy like the top of a freshly-baked fruit crumble, uneven underfoot, the molehill summits capped white with frost like miniature Andean volcanoes. Sunshine is sharp, throwing tight shadows and glinting off iced floodwater. In places, that ice glimmers opaquely where gas has become trapped from the grass still photosynthesising beneath it. Three male mallards swim on a pond, quacking softly, nasally, their movements maintaining a black gaping abyss in the water, free from the encroaching frost-dusted ice upon which another pair stand. Familiarity and hybridisation have led to their disregard, yet when they stand on orange legs with their white-ringed necks stretched high holding bottle-green heads and yellow bills aloft, maroon breasts and white-bordered shining blue specula and incongruously kiss-curled tails, their intricate beauty is a match for that of most wildfowl. In the fields, the sheep do not graze; instead they huddle and nibble at the tall bleached, dead grass in the hedges while waiting for the sun to thaw their pastures. In this white landscape there is even white on white, for the sheep bear crusts of frost on their wool. A few browse the dark green ovals from which they have risen after spending the night. Greenfinches haunt gnarled skeletal hedges. A buzzard alights nearby, accompanied by its ever-present retinue of raucous black avian paparazzi that seem to delight in tormenting it.

A dog fox forages for food amongst the frozen grasses, trotting nonchalantly across the fields, head swinging back and forth, pulled this way and that by his nose seeking some sort of sustenance however meagre. His pelage is thick and wiry, wet and dark and sleek, his brush lush and lavish and imitating a weathervane, for he wraps it close around his body when moving west with the wind behind him but holds it straight out when he turns in the opposite direction. A smell yanks him back: he returns to thoroughly sniff an otherwise unprepossessing area of grass. He rootles determinedly into the base of the tussocks, deep in his world of scents, oblivious to all around him, snuffling busily and scratching with both paws, yet he unearths nothing and resumes his path. He comes to a fence. The posts are adorned by a chorus line of six magpies. He looks closely, weighing up the likelihood of being able to leap up and catch one. His body language imparts recognition of the futility of such an option, yet the lack of alternatives and the closeness of the birds imbue hope. He gazes up imploringly. He moves forward and the birds remain. He moves forward again, to beneath his chosen post. The magpie gazes down. The fox tenses to spring and the magpie leisurely flutters up, moving left, displacing its neighbour. They all ripple along like can-can dancers and the futility of his task springs shut on him. He turns and moves away, zigzagging across the field, causing some lapwings to rise like snow ghosts, squealing as if making a plea for mercy. They take two wingbeats before landing a metre away in the frozen grass, just enough energy expended to register their alertness to the fox.

Slowly, the sun peels back the frost to reveal a green and ochre land-scape, the thawing surface now curiously soft underfoot like putty. A thou-sand golden plover rise into the lucidity of the upper air, buoyant on their mournful whistles wafted on the wind, drifting like black snowflakes; yet when the sun lights them they glitter golden against the dark of a rising cloud like the golden spangles of their own plumage, repeated patterns at different scales. They cease their wingbeats and become masters of the glide, floating lightly on the breeze, descending leisurely, lingering in the beauty of flight, reticent to make landfall. They turn slowly but not in tight unison like dunlin, instead rippling lazily back and forth as if blown by eddies, all the while showering the fields below with their soft piping calls, an effervescent sound that somehow seems to expand the very air around them. A small flock of chaffinches flush from the grass, flashing white in their wings and tails like snowflakes stirred up by a swirling gust of wind.

While the rest of the world waits for spring, in a rough pasture a male stock dove courts his love with unabashed vivacity. He puffs out his neck feathers, green and purple and iridescent like a sheen of petrol on water, and bows, raising his fanned tail, then stumbles through the grass and bows again and again and again. The female, apparently bored, flaps into the air on softly clapping wings, the male in close pursuit. She lands back in the field and the male bows. She flies to a wall and the male bows. She lands on a gate and the male bows; and bows and bows and bows. A fieldfare watches from a bush, the wrong side of a long journey to yet have such lust in mind.

The day is wet. Light falls dull under a veil of mist, the cloud low, the drizzle intermittent. The land, opaque with muted definition and colours, drifts to a faint translucent horizon like a sun-bleached photograph. Overhead, the zesty piping of a lone oystercatcher sounds above the ceaseless symphony of the waves, all exuberant excitement then sudden silence. The tide is retreating, setting free the curlews from the boredom of their shoreline roost. They fly as one in a flurry of wings to spread across the mud, their source of life. A flock of dunlin, high in the greyness, tumble suddenly like rain before regrouping inches above the mud to resume their westward progress.

Light dims, the cloud descends, and the eastern hills fade away as the horizon foreshortens. The landscape becomes more intimate, the sky flattens, the distant holm floats on an aqueous horizon like a marooned ship set adrift from the coast now invisible in the banks of cloud behind it. The glistening mud is re-absorbed slowly into the thickening fog. Flocks of waders coalesce at favoured points to resume their frantic feeding; dunlin, grey plover and knot, busy living along the edge, flying frequently from half-imagined danger before returning to the same point. A group of redshank land on the upper shore, each of them stretching its wings vertically before folding them away as if needing to flush excess flight from their feathers before commencing ground-based activity. Common gulls stand well apart from each other, preening unconcernedly, seeming to prefer their own company to that of their larger irascible congeners scattered in groups amongst the waders. Close to shore, turning over the scattered debris of the stranded tide wrack, is a turnstone with whimsical orange legs glowing in the gloom.

Still the horizon creeps nearer, the holm gone now, sunk in the expanse of grey; the down is barely discernible as a dark suggestion through the cloud, then it too disappears into the deepening murk. A male kestrel hovers over the coast path on quivering chestnut wings, pale grey tail fanned, unaware and unconcerned of the landscape vanishing around it. Its head is motionless, focused solely on the grass below, where its ultraviolet vision will allow the urine-marked runs of the territorial voles it hunts to be as clearly visible to it as a road atlas is to humans, easing the location of its prey. As the horizon closes further, the knoll becomes the latest casualty, now invisible in the enveloping mist. The far riverbank and island remain the only solid points of reference, but even the edges of these are softening as the first cold vapour tickles and coalesces on the skin; then these too are lost as the world is reduced to a blank canvas, as if the landscape had never been. Time ceases. Only sound remains – the strident yelping of the herring gulls echoing from the lost shore, the mournful pleadings of the plovers, the wistfulness of the redshanks' whistles chiming off the glassy air, and from the far distance the heartache of the curlews' tremolos.

Haltingly, the landscape reforms. As slowly as it retreated, the horizon now advances – the riverbank reforming, the knoll sharpening out of the mist; the down coalescing to solidity; the holm rising phoenix-like once more from the waves. The birds disperse across the lengthening ribs of the mud, their calls muting as the distance grows; the skyward dancing flocks have gone. Suddenly, behind all, the cloud breaks and the western hills bloom in the spring sunshine, the green fields capped by the purple moorland and dotted with the white buds of the farmhouses, like snowdrops on the hills.

The rising tide is rushing. Noisy. As the sun clears the eastern horizon waves are turned frosted pink as if the pigment from the clouds has been washed into the water by the rain. The sun now rises from directly behind the church tower as it progresses relentlessly along the horizon each morning towards the apex of its summer solstice somewhere far away to the north-east and June. As morning unfolds, cumuli tower, a sky of interlocking cold whites and greys and icy blues like a baroque canopy of hallowed scenes. The sun is warm, the clouds drift. Light and shadow lace the sea. Dull steely greys are flat and lifeless, swallowing the motion of the waves; vibrant sepias and ochres are full of movement; the changes pulsing across the water like those across the body of a squid. On land, the saltmarsh gleams like baize upon which the silvered fretwork of interlaced flood pools is displayed. Fields are radiant, light dances off green, deep in tone yet superficial in time, vanishing with the returning cloud shadows, glimpses of spring eclipsed by winter's obstinance. Two foxes canter across the grass, tails held straight out behind. The dog follows the vixen's every turn, maintaining a set distance, increasing his pace only immediately after passing through a hedge or under a gate to make up lost ground. A female merlin alights on a concrete cattle trough and leans deeply in to drink from the dark water. From amongst the ripples, death stares back. The merlin's footing slips, but with fluttering wings and a helping hand from the breeze, she rises clear and settles on the broader cowling. She pauses, but thirst remains; it returns her to the slippery lip where she sips again from the edge of the abyss, thirty centimetres deep and an eternity. She slips again and death rises, clutching close. It soaks cold into her thigh feathers and pulls. Her wings splash the surface but she is strong enough to beat free of its grasp. Danger now recognised, she flickers away fast and low before pulling sharply upwards into wind to rest atop the swaying twigs of a hawthorn.

In long grass at the edge of the riverbank path, a sparrowhawk is disturbed with a recent kill. It has ambushed a dunlin in one of the deep tidal gutters and carried it here. The hawk's eyes flare with fear of the human and hatred of the acute predicament posed by this chance encounter, that of remaining with its hard-won meal or of fleeing without it. Its dilemma is apparent in the delay before its own flight, a delay that could have cost it its own life. The dunlin remains, its headless corpse still warm, a smudge of red the only blemish on its white breast where the first feathers have been plucked. Its legs are still now, its wings neatly folded, its energy gone, its calls silenced. Close by, six redshanks feed in a shallow pool, swimming daintily, twisting like phalaropes to snatch small insects from the surface. A little egret lands in a flurry of steps and spray, and the redshank flush, flicking away low across the marsh with singularly light flight, a mixture of fast wingbeats and long glides, frictionless like a skater gliding across ice, their anguished calls receding like lost souls departing for the River Styx.

A still day in February, a rare jewel. The eastern hills lie swaddled under grey clouds but overhead, wedges of blue are forcing them apart. Despite the cold and the lingering frosts, and despite the wind, and despite the many grey wet days to come, spring is stepping slowly from the shadows of winter. Days are lengthening, the clarity of the light increasing as the sun climbs higher in the sky. This day is the first spring-like day of the year, yet it is not spring, just a happy interlude: a trailer for spring advertising all the best bits but making no promises as to when it will premiere, for the gentle southerly breeze still bears a keen edge. Birdsong is stuttering into life. All around, the sharp two-tone repetitions of great tits ring across the fields. A wren trills brightly, trailing off abruptly as if its clockwork has run down, needing to be rewound before the next song can be delivered. A dunnock sings its thin tuneless ditty from a fence post. A skylark makes its first ascent of the year, a wake of sparkling semi-quavers dropping in the air below him. He flies not high, for this is just a first rehearsal, and these mercurial baubles of sound will be linked and polished to a scintillant iridescence by the time of the lengthy soliloquys of his main performances in April. They sliver down to meld with the first short bars from a robin in the brambles, its song now changed from autumn's regretful hesitancy to springtime verve. A female kestrel juts atop a stunted naked ash, her rich rufous plumage lustrous in the still austere surroundings, the sunshine accentuating the yellow orbital ring around the black wetness of her iris. A dozen fieldfares and four redwings forage in the sheep pasture below, migrants much too wily to be beguiled into commencing homeward journeys by just one deceptive sunny morning.

In the bay, dunlin surge from the mud in a rolling wave like a newspaper lifting in the wind, before settling once more. Echelons of golden plovers drizzle north-east. Wader numbers have declined since autumn, the depredations of the raptors and the ravages of winter's cold and furies have depleted them, leaving Darwin's survivors to make the journey north once more to mould each species' future. In the shallows of a lagoon, three hundred curlews stand serene, curved bills sheathed under wings, waiting calmly and patiently for the sea's retreat, while behind them more dunlin boil back and forth over its surface. Suddenly waders and gulls and wildfowl convulse as one into the softness of the chill air in a chaos of wings. Yet no peregrine appears, no merlin materialises, no harrier heaves into view. Half a minute later a low-flying naval helicopter churns over the bay, splintering the wind with the deafening rhythmic thump of its rotors. Calm returns warily for some. Lapwings spiral down to the saltmarsh, parachuting on open wings with legs trailing, the air seemingly now too frail to support them further, but the curlews do not return. On the river, the sparkling silver water merges seamlessly with the sparkling silver mud, the boundary marked solely by a narrow dark beading of redshanks feeding along the edge. A cormorant cruises by, brief glides interspersing its robust flapping, black plumage now adorned by a white thigh patch of courtship plumage. Gulls stutter querulously overhead, ever fractious. In the sea couch-grass the first of the yellow dung-flies are emerging from their diapause, torpid and clumsy and greedy for sunshine. Early swarms of gnats undulate over brambles, untroubled by the light breeze. Slowly the blue fades as a grey coverlet of cloud creeps across the sky. The light dulls. Songs still. The skylark makes its final descent, the dunnock's hurried ramblings cease. Spring is back on hold, survival again the order of the day as the cold rain once more slants across the fields.

The shadow from the floodbanks stretches slowly out across the saltmarsh towards the river as the sun dips westward. In the hedge along the base of the bank, the buds on the violet-umber thorns are still clamped tightly shut. Only low down in shelter are the first compound leaflets of an elder emerging, soft and fresh, and as vivid green as only fresh chlorophyll can be. A wren forages amongst the faded stems of last summer's willowherb, bent and broken, slanting from the onslaught of the winter's storms. It bursts into a staccato of alarm, bouncing on jelly legs, full of apprehension, ceasing calling as it dives down into the depths of the tangled vegetation. Woodpigeons waddle heavily through the fields, clipping the heads of the newly-growing grass, selecting favoured stems with care. Their pale cream irides bestow on them a wide-eyed vacant look; whenever they look up they appear startled, as if uncomprehending. Lapwings have become more combative as spring nears. Tetchy and intolerant, they chase each other on the ground and in the air, their laconic calls now replaced with petulance and infused with an effervescent buzzy squeak like a baby's old-fashioned rubber dolly. They will leave shortly for the tilled lands and rough grazing to the north and east.

As the sun ignites the few remaining clouds high over the river, fronds of dunlin fold through the sky heading for the mudflats, braids of golden plover high above them, differential distance equalising size, silhouettes against the rising brightness of the sky making all of them black and starling-like. In the last rays of the setting sun, a peregrine planes across the fields on level wings kindling birds from the grass and hedgerows. A hundred slack-winged lapwings let out a collective squeal as they lift from the grass. Woodpigeons clatter from bushes; thrushes scold. A solitary mallard rises from a rhyne. Starlings smoke into the light, whirling on the eddies of the falcon's wake while it weaves between them with blissful insouciance, slipping one way then the other. But the birds have everything to fear, and blind instinct drives them to defence – lapwings climb flapping loosely, woodpigeons laboriously twist and turn, thrushes dive back into cover, starlings clump and wheel – for well they must since behind the benign nonchalance the peregrine is probing, seeking any weakness that would identify a quarry. A slight feint to startle, to separate, and suddenly the real thing; a slight rise into wind and with a drop of its wing it sideslips, lunging through the heart of the woodpigeon flock with raking talons, missing, and skimming out low over the bleached reeds fringing the riverbank. The smoke thins, the turmoil subsides, the fields and bushes fill, but the cloying sense of fear remains … always the fear remains.

Night comes moonless but clear and star-spangled, their light shimmering in the crispness of the fast-cooling air. Winter still owns the darkness. The ground is hardening. From the gaunt branches of the walnut tree behind the house, invisible in the silky blackness, a little owl calls its endlessly repetitive single whistle. Flat but echoing, hollow and toneless, it is infinitely monotonous, like a radar blip pulsing into the ether of the frosty night, waiting for a response to echo back that will signal the first signs of a possible mate. Does it hope while it is calling? Does it register a rush of expectancy that fuels that hope, and despair when another night ends in silence? Or is it really just a feathered automaton forlornly pumping out its call, a prisoner of its genes?

This is what he has been waiting for, the waiting bird: silky blue skies, the sun warm on skin and feather, the light sharp, the shadows crisp. Thermals are rising, flagged by small white cumulus clouds turning grey beneath as they grow, a spring day inserted into the endless grey of February. No longer confined to the wet fields, the excruciating boredom of the fenceposts under flat grey skies and the squalor of searching for earthworms in the mud and the rain, the buzzard is free to fly once more. He circles tightly, tucked into the pillar of buoyant air, wings thrown forward embracing the lift, relishing the pleasure of the commonplace in a way that is only possible after prolonged absence has made it uncommon, like recovery after illness or injury. The land that has held him through the shackles of winter recedes below him. The horizon expands and curves. The silver meniscus of the sea enlarges to the north. As he reaches the thermal's capstone, he can climb no further and rolls out of his turn, sloughing off the cloud's shadow, blinking in the sunlit air, luxuriating in its bright warmth. But the exuberance at being free to fly again demands more than gentle gliding, commands greater exhilaration, requires celebration. The buzzard half-closes his wings, sleeks his tail and begins to tip forward, slowly at first but gradually accelerating as the angle of his fall increases. He drops several hundred feet sheer before he opens his wings again, slowly, trading speed for lift, rising sharply to the top of a curve, now only a little below where he started his dive, riding the cusp of the stall, then closing his wings once more, falling and rising, falling and rising; and as each dive becomes a climb he calls, like a child screaming at the sudden change in G-force on a fairground rollercoaster; a high-pitched cat-like mewing, wild, echoing, and ethereal, the sound of the wooded valleys in the distant high country.

All rollercoasters run out of energy, and at five hundred feet he spreads his wings and glides to refuel in another thermal, banking again into a slow ascending spiral that will elevate him back to the upper air, there to begin his display once more. Scientific logic would ascribe such display to the start of breeding; a simple convergence of rising hormones and fine weather, and undoubtedly in part it is. Although buzzards do not breed here, for there are no suitable trees, other species also display or sing here while just migrating through. Yet in the move to rightly discredit anthropomorphism perhaps the pendulum has swung too far, for the idea that animals lack all emotion seems as perverse as the idea that birds sing because they are happy. Tempting it may be to believe that birds live in the here and now, to interpret their existence as being only in the present – the moment, now, being everything, the past a clouded nothingness, the

110

future incomprehensible. And yet … and yet Manx shearwaters know their nest burrows exist across the far side of an ocean and can find them with pinpoint accuracy, albatrosses perform elaborate greetings to their mates over a lifetime together, an owl mourns its dead mate for days by the roadside where it was killed by a car. A mechanistic response within an evolutionary architecture undoubtedly – and yet … and yet with a memory and even a rudimentary feel of a future, the basic construct for meaning above mere sentience is in place, and with meaning an ability to respond to it: emotion. And a gradual cline of meaning through the evolutionary tree has to be more plausible than some tectonic fault line between those with it – humans – and those perceived by some to be without it. And so the buzzard displays: not only a pre-programmed ritual for attracting a mate but also a performance of boundless joy, when it flies not because it needs to, not because it can, but because it simply wants to

.

MARCH
THE WRONG SIDE OF THE WORLD

A lone curlew pipes in a candy floss dawn melting over icing sugar fields. Clouds swirl upward ahead of another cold front, dazzling in the low sunshine of early spring. Clouds swirl downward from cows' breath condensing around their muzzles. The morning is hushed, the wind not quite still, the peace broken only by the familiar soft conversation between sea and shore. This is the quietest time of year. Bird numbers, exhausted from the winter, are at their lowest, not yet boosted by the arrival of summer migrants nor replenished through breeding. Yet thoughts are turning to that. Skylarks are lifting from the shoreline cord-grass, trailing vestiges of song into the transparent blue sky, increasingly complex fragments being tried and linked into precursors of the intricate traceries that will come later in the spring; the song flights themselves still short and low. Great tits stammer their strident two-tone songs amongst the shifting shadows of the bare willows, while along the hedges dunnocks sing their loud but tinny warbles, insubstantial renditions that end abruptly as if the birds have forgotten the final bars. Only a single chaffinch, perched in the highest leafless branch of a bush, is in full song; its repetitive tune, full-polished and merry, sung with brio but all alone, for its congeners continue to squabble for seed at various feeders within the village.

On the foreshore, a female merlin perches atop an ancient post. Her worn upperparts glow with the rich brown of freshly-turned autumn sod, her eye lustrous sable beneath a pale arched supercilium. She rests, yet is clearly restless, toes kneading the furrowed wood, wings fidgeting, body feathers alternately fluffed and sleeked. She raises a foot to her beak and nibbles between the toes, then turns a half-circle, displaying clean white underparts with neat brown streaking. She bobs occasionally, and turns half-circle once more, her head now cocking from side to side. She raises her tail and suddenly pitches forward, lunging into the air with a powerful thrust of her yellow legs. She races low across the glaucous grass and blue pools, shallow wingbeats flicking the air away behind her, rising over a lagoon bank and snatching haphazardly at the air which a skylark has just vacated. She turns sharply, empty-footed, and glides back from whence she came; a flight without obvious focus, perhaps simply a need to flush excess energy from her body.

Just above the incoming tide, four bar-tailed godwits roost amongst a group of curlews. They stand on one leg, twisting gently back and forth like a weathervane in a variable wind to maximise their field of view, sleeping only in tiny snatches, eyes never closed for more than a few seconds, the need for watchfulness ever present. An errant crow shudders them into full wakefulness – four long, slightly upturned bills unsheathed from beneath wings, their bases an incongruous princess-pink complementing the otherwise cold tones of their grey, brown, and buff plumage. The rising tide makes them increasingly agitated, their shorter legs posing them an intractable dilemma between the need for flight ahead of the deepening water and the safety bequeathed by remaining within the flock of taller curlews to which the tide poses no imminent threat. The godwits hop shoreward, curiously reluctant to withdraw their other leg from within their body plumage. Yet the curlews' irritation with this increasing motion disturbing their slumber is palpable, aggressive posturing rippling through the semi-slumbering flock like snoozing adults admonishing thoughtless children. Nearby, four redshanks balance on a drift log like vermilion-legged acrobats, while in the still water of the flooded lagoon roosting wader numbers are doubled by their reflections. High above, golden plover stardust scattered against the muted blue sky weaves in diffuse flocks, its musical wheedling melting into the wind, loud then soft, as if drifting in and out of focus, the edges of the arriving and departing sound uncertain, leaving the listener unsure as to whether it has really been heard at all.

Spring beguiles. A light frosting is testament to forgotten winds, itself soon erased in the radiance of the morning sun. Chiffon blue billows limitless above and dazzles from flooded fields, the legacy of incessant rains. A heron watches its reflection in the reflection of its eye in the water below. In the drier parts of hay meadows, shorn of their winter-grazing sheep since the start of the month, cowslips are pushing their pale yellow candelabras above crinkled leaves, the elongated corollas unfolding just above the top of the still short but growing grass. The first few bees already bumble between them. Over a pond, the swollen buds of goat willows are erupting into silky silver catkins.

In one, a few wistful whistles give way to an early cadence of spring as the slipping repetitions of the first chiffchaff proclaims its presence. In years past this was one of the first spring migrants, but although it now overwinters in England it is rarely present on the peninsula past early December, so it heralds spring even if it hasn't come far. It is a green-washed buff with a cream supercilium and a hint of yellow on the bend of the wing, veiled with a tracery of shadows from the sunlit branches above. It flies abruptly, but only upwards amongst the buds, there to continue its song, occasionally sallying forth to catch alder flies floating in small swarms in the lee of the trees.

In the drier fields, the new lambs are out for the first time, small and inquisitive, with heads too big for their bodies and floppy ears bouncing as they run and skip on still-wobbly legs. Insatiably curious, they investigate everything, nibbling at inedible dead stems and the wire fences, the attractions of grass not yet of interest. Their umbilical cords are shrivelled but still present, as are their long tails, which still follow their exuberant and uninhibited skipping, or quiver in uncontrolled ecstasy while feeding on mothers' warm milk; but the elastic bands encircling their tails are working inexorably towards their separation from their owners. Somewhere over a distant field a skylark sings at the limit of hearing, a tracery of glittering sound embroidering the edge of morning. The quicksilver rush of a sparrowhawk blurs along the base of a hedge, coasting past dark hawthorns still tight with winter, and old elders whose smooth pale grey branches are softened and smudged by bright yellow lichen drawn close around them like an overcoat. It steals through the dappled light, an insubstantial shadow melding with those around it, gliding long, flapping infrequently, cruising attentively, ever looking for that opportunity. In the sunshine of the open grass, a hare sitting up on its haunches watches the hawk passing before resuming cleaning its long soft ears. Satisfactorily primped, it engages in a bout of shadow boxing, rearing up on its hindquarters and jabbing rapidly with its front paws, all the while bouncing backwards and circling, focusing its efforts on a particular point of empty air ahead of itself, practising for the important matches soon to come. Nearby, on a field gate, a male woodpigeon is oblivious to all around except his potential mate, to whom he raises his tail in graceful arcs, the first offerings towards a promise of a summer to be spent together.

A calm between two storms, a calm between two seasons; the quiet peninsula almost seems to be resting, yet change is all around. The tatters of winter are being shed. The air is crisp and almost frosted, sunlight leaking through a diaphanous layer of high stratus. A moorhen draws a narrow dark line through the dew as it forages on the short grass by a pond. Two ravens cruise low over the fields, rolling resonant Rs conversationally between them, disturbing a pair of magpies searching expectantly for docked lambs' tails. Above in the brightness, a sparrowhawk displays, circling high, soaring like imagination. Linnets have returned, birds rarely seen at this end of the village in winter. Their twittering is strangely unfamiliar after their months away but, together with their incessant flitting, reinvigorates the hedges. Meadow pipit flocks have been passing through the fields in recent days, the air full of their insipid calls. The reedbeds are awakening, the repetitive seedy sound of a reed bunting emanating from deep in the tawny haze. The call has a spiv-like quality to it, sharp and attention-grabbing, 'tsikk' – like the prelude to ' 'ere, Guv, wanna buy a watch?'– the bird itself, perched on a reed stem bowed under its weight, looking like some sharply dressed gangster with black hat and white scarf. Beyond, the mudflats are nearly empty; a couple of puffs of dunlin swirl over the incoming sea, the last remnants of the smoking multitudes of autumn, like the final wisps from a dying bonfire. Most of the winter waders have departed; the dunlin have danced northwards; the curlews, answering the call of the wild moorlands, have bid farewell; the lapwings left as one overnight a week ago, as sure a sign of winter's passing as the arrival of swallows heralding the arrival of summer. The silver-dappled saltmarsh is largely empty, just a scattering of large gulls loafing by the draining tidal pools. Three cormorants hulk on the edge of the riverbank, their angularity making them strangely mechanical, as if cut from pieces of metal and bolted together. A little egret breaks its flight, angling sharply down to a pool to greet its arriving reflection.

In one of the lagoons, flooded by the last high tide, a flock of shelduck shine in the cloud-veiled sunlight of mid-morning. Serenity pervades the surface with birds sleeping and loafing and preening, but a frisson of tension underlies it for hormones are rising and displaying has commenced. Frequently a male will rear up to full height, extending his bottle-green neck and head, and throwing his vibrant scarlet bill upwards, flicking it in the air repeatedly in a syncopated action while crooning, occasionally accompanying this by beating his open wings. Each then settles sheepishly, yet this is mock rest, for each bird is acutely aware of the proximity of others, the head-raising display of one setting off chains of imitations running through the flock. Sometimes, these descend into open hostility with an aggressor rushing forward with hunched shoulders, neck extended, head lowered, and tail wagging vigorously while the object of its ire beats a hasty retreat until a satisfactory distance has been re-established between the two. Most of this is posturing, for very shortly after having been forced to retreat, a bird can be seen to settle close to its assailant again without further belligerence. While most females are still indifferent to the males' antics, some have begun to pair, allowing an intimacy that others are seeking to achieve. A male seeks to reassure his mate with gentle circular motions of his head, drawing it backwards and down onto his mantle before throwing it quickly forwards in a rising then falling curve, quacking softly and gutturally, while the female sometimes responds with gentle excited whiffling whistles, building the bond between them. For other females, indifference is sometimes not enough, and having failed to deter their amorous suitors they take refuge in the air on faintly whispering wings with three or four males still in pursuit, twisting away across the saltmarsh to land amongst another flock, there triggering ripples of fresh displays.

The wind is ferocious. For three days it has pummelled the peninsula. And still it blows, unquenchable, relentless, wearing. The wind vane swings rapidly back and forth between west and north-west. The sea roars in the bay. White horses break far out on the pale brown barrelling waves, running long and fast towards the shore. The seaward horizon is hazy, heavy with salt spray. Light is dynamic. Blue skies change to violet-black backdrops and back again. Dazzling white clouds race overhead, giving birth to fleeting rainbows as their showers slant across the bay. Reeds are agitated, fretting and fussing in a flurry of constant motion. Sunlight shimmers on their swaying heads like ripened barley. The low tangled brambles shuffle and twitch in the gusts, while the tall arching briar stems wave and thrash above. Sheep and their lambs huddle in the lee of the biggest bushes in the hedges. Walking is difficult; flight a trial. A magpie careens across the fields, long tail blown almost ahead of itself, struggling to maintain coordination. Perversely, some snatches of a skylark's song briefly pervade the wind, the bird singing just a couple of feet above the reedbed before dropping quickly back down into shelter.

Along the lane, mud is soft and sucking, squelching underfoot. Puddles splash. Blackthorn flower buds are just breaking, bright like early morning dew. One of the willows has lost a limb. The gash is raw and ragged, the torn timber fresh cream, the broken bark pale orange around the fracture, both bright against the grey-green smoothness of the uninjured bole. The broken limb lies across the track, shattered wood all around, small branches and twigs scattered in the brambles. A little egret flushes from the shelter of the nearby rhyne. It is grounded immediately it clears the bank, the wind catching it and knocking it sideways, its legs and wings akimbo as it staggers to stay standing. It looks around confused, unsure of what to do since its innate ability for reflex flight has been unexpectedly removed. It runs a few metres through the short grass, looking back over its shoulder, trying to ascertain the danger it initially perceived. Two black crows, jagged with feathers splayed by the wind, interrupt their feeding to watch it before returning to forage, thickset and bull-like, muscling through the grass. A single starling flies across the open fields directly into the wildness, its compact bullet shape providing aerial prowess.

Cloud shadows sashay across the saltmarsh, which is full of shelduck displaced from the churning sea. Most are clamped tight onto the grass, sitting heads under wings, along with a number of large gulls in similar repose. Only a few are dabbling in pools; all face north-west into the gale. The lagoons are empty. Sparkling ripples on their surface make regular patterns like frosted grass, growing larger as they cross the water, leaping over the windward bank in spurts of spray. Overhead, a meadow pipit is lost in the wind, having been plucked from its ill-considered flight and flung skywards into the maelstrom. Tossed and thrown by the capricious tumult, its power of controlled flight has been snatched away and the force of gravity negated as it tumbles skywards. There, alone in its distress, struggling to return to land, it is suddenly assaulted. A female merlin looms out of the blue, condensing like an apparition, yet real and malevolent. She closes fast, trying to take advantage of the waif's predicament, wings beating hard and with its tail making reflexive adjustments to maintain its desired course through the battering air. Yet the tempest that has tossed the pipit into a paroxysm is also its saviour, for the precise manoeuvring required by the merlin to bring her close enough to snatch the pipit from the sky has been removed in the lottery of the gale. The merlin rises sharply, loops the loop, and dives again from slightly above and behind, misses and arcs around to come in level from the side, but overshoots. Defeated by the jinking pipit and the buffeting air, she curves around in front of her quarry and tries to intercept it head-on, slowing into the wind, but the pipit blows straight past it and the chase resumes, the two birds now far out across the river, embraced in a grotesque parody of a ballet, the denouement known only to the participants for they are lost to view in the white haze of distance on the towering wind.

The wind in the willows sighs, and on its southerly caress come sand martins on rapidly fluttering wings, the first migrants carrying the spring. Small and fast, their flight is direct with a strangely frenetic quality, for unlike swallows they rarely seem to glide. They will not linger here, for there is nowhere for them to breed and for them it is not the beginning of spring; it is not the beginning of anything; it is not even the end of their journey, for they have many more miles to go. But over the peninsula their fleeting presence is a welcome sign of the ascent of spring – independent travellers ahead of the hordes of package tourists still to come. Yet the weather belies this promise, as is so often the case in a month when such contradictions abound, for the day is grey and chilly after the recent rain, the weak sun occasionally bright but bereft of warmth. The dark blue hills hulking to the east, fringed by the bare mauve branches of trees swelling with rising sap, provide the perfect foil for the graceful flight of a little egret blinking fluorescent white like a strobe light. In the distance, a large flock of feeding woodpigeons casts a muted purple haze across a meadow. A male greenfinch wheezes repetitively, its protracted dry rasping seeming to require lubrication. In the shining grass of a wet pasture two hares sit erect, long black ears twitching as they watch a dog fox trot by not two hundred metres away, confident in their speed to evade it. The fox is similarly knowledgeable, yet it cannot help but cast a covetous gaze at them as it moves by. Three skylarks levitate on quavering wings to hold a singing contest low over the wet field while cattle stand nearby like a panel waiting to judge each contestant's performance. Before then, decorum degenerates into fracas as the soloist objects to the backing singers and chases them with pugilistic abandon. The cattle, now uninterested, return to feeding on the short but sprouting grass, no longer huddled in the muddy squalor of the shelter of the hedges to which the wind seems to have confined them for most of the winter. In another meadow, a lamb bleats with distress, lost on the wrong side of its field – the wrong side of the world. Although its mother calls back, low and calm and rolling, this fails to soothe her offspring, her audible presence but visual absence simply compounding the lamb's anguish and escalating its high-pitched panic. The ewe ceases feeding and begins the long trek across the field to rescue it, a journey shortened when the lamb finally catches sight of her and races so fast across the last gap between them that it nearly trips over its own legs on its way to suckle. No longer does its tail bounce and quiver as it feeds, for like most of the lambs now it has lost it. The elastic bands have done their work, the tails have dropped, the magpies have feasted. Yet grazing the grass still holds little appeal against suckling the rich warmth of mother's milk; or a doze in the warmth of early spring sunshine; or king-of-the-castle on top of the ancient ruined walls; or a game of chase, skipping and jumping around the fields in rambunctious gangs. Sun shining through pink ears; pink noses on soft white faces; their cute innocence will soon be lost to the bonier growth of adulthood.

Sunbeams cant through the slowly shifting clouds. The shoreline is quiet. The mud to the east is pale tawny in the bright sunshine, stretching away like a desert; the sea so far out on the tide that it has ceased to be. To the west, with the harsh white glare of the afternoon as a backdrop, it is dark; long ribs lying like fallen basalt columns between glistening silver pools stretching infinitely into the distance. The horizon is the mud. Everything beyond is swallowed by haze. Over the low sand ridge between the mud and the reedbed, two ringed plovers court, circling on wings flicked deliberately in slow motion, wild tremulous piping oscillating around them. They land, shuffling feathers, and return to feed.

Over the saltmarsh, a lone curlew flees the haunting desolation of its call. Amongst the taller grasses a hare zig-zags through the tussocks, nimble and poised, fast but not frantic. Behind, chasing hard, a fox gains steadily, striding long, ears flattened, tail streaming behind it; its seemingly easy gait belied by hard breathing. The gap shrinks, the hare's evasion tactics ineffective, the fox now obviously too close for comfort, for the hare suddenly accelerates, straightening its course, spurting forwards, sprinting away as those long hind legs it drags around behind it during quiet feeding, abruptly power its body forwards and up into the air. It lands fleetingly on its front paws as, with deeply flexing spine, its rear legs overlap its front, pounding the ground hard, extending once more to take it airborne again. All the while it holds its long ears curiously erect. Pursuer recedes rapidly from pursued and the fox abruptly breaks off, exhausted, coming to rest panting raggedly, its flanks heaving as it gulps down lungfuls of air. The hare slows and lollops into cover, its long hind legs once more seemingly a burden.

Evening comes later now the days are lengthening. In the golden bubble of last light before the grey-cowled chill of dusk usurps it, a short-eared owl slips silently along the base of a hedgerow. It flies slowly, deep sensuous beats of its long wings stroking the air as if it were velvet, interspersed with protracted gentle glides, boxing with its shadow as it hugs the ground. In its wake, a trail of dissonant alarm calls rises out of the silent eddies of its passage; blackbirds and great tits, robins and wrens, scolding from the bushes. The owl doubles back, dropping sharply with long feathered legs outstretched, crumpling in slow motion as it impacts the ground, but is airborne again quickly, for there is no time to muse on missed opportunities. It continues to drift over the tall grass fringing the hedgerows, folding itself into the vegetation again and again, yet only on the fifth attempt does it stay down much longer, partially hidden from view but clearly swallowing a small mammal. Then once more it is on the wing, quartering the field randomly with erratic changes of direction. It floats out over the fussing seed heads of the reeds that refract auburn haloes from the rays of the dying sunlight. Distantly, the last liquid canticles of a blackbird cease. The owl condenses from its languid flight onto a drift-branch on the foreshore and looks back over its shoulder as if it knows it is being watched, itself watching the watcher, its molten yellow eyes set deep in the crater of its facial disc. It blinks once and slowly turns away.

As the sun rises higher, the clarity of the morning light becomes sullied by shadows from the germinating clouds. The wind has finally turned, still blowing, but warmer now it is from the south. Fast clouds produce fast light. The fields switch constantly between sunshine and shade. Sparkles skip across the surface of pools. A buzzard circles on the breeze with never a flap, just small alterations in attitude, tilting a wing gently to counter an air pocket, rocking softly in loose ellipses, sometimes pausing hanging over a point, sometimes making several loops in quick succession, ever drifting downwind. A heron crosses the fields towards the saltmarsh, flying with heavy elegance imparted by purposeful wing beats. Lark song expands the sky. The birds sing effortlessly in virtuoso performances in the azure voids between the clouds, like kites tethered to the ground by molten threads of song, the ear mesmerised by the tumbling cascades long before the eye can find the right focal plane to pick out the singer dancing in the aerial arena high above. There is an urgency to the torrent of bubbling notes as if spring is too late or summer just too short for all their songs.

From within a bower of frothy blackthorn blossom, a wren delivers its compelling song, the strident trilling bursting forth as if the sound is too much to be contained within its small frame, and the finish abrupt as if the pressure has been exhausted like in a deflating balloon. Below the hedge where the first of the flowers have fallen like flecks of foam, two male blackbirds are fighting over a territorial boundary known only to them, like black-clad ninjas battling ferociously, leaping, lunging, and lancing with golden katanas. In the lane, a brown hare approaches slowly like temptation, its long back legs reluctantly following its front ones. It stops and quivers its nostrils, its long white whiskers feeling the air currents in a parody of a snake's tongue, huge black-tipped ears alert and trembling, rich amber irides deep wells of wariness. It relaxes slightly, enough to draw back and up onto its haunches, exposing its white belly. It licks its front paws and begin to groom its damp fur, pulling one paw cat-like along the top of an ear bent forward. It stops and tenses, aware of human presence but although it appears unable to comprehend the stillness of the human form despite its close proximity, it is suspicious enough to retreat. It turns and lopes leisurely back down the lane, like temptation met with conscience.

The final day of March, and the shipping forecast, 'Lundy. Northwest severe gale nine, backing west, increasing storm force ten. Squally showers becoming heavy rain. Moderate, becoming poor', has now fully arrived as another ferocious equinoctial storm pounds the peninsula. The roar of the sea merges with that of the screaming wind. The low pressure of the storm seems to have raised the sea and the wind bludgeons it landward, piling it upward towards the shore. Rank upon rank of mountainous waves emerge through the rain, each appearing to be higher than the land itself. The horizon bulges in a gentle curve. It looks as if the sea will easily overwhelm the fragile line of the aged shingle sea defences. Yet when each frothing wave arrives in a rush across the flooded saltmarsh, it dissipates harmlessly through the fringing reedbed, sloughing off its energy, slumping away its height through the stones of the coast path, its optical illusion fully revealed. Along the path, displaced snipe erupt sequentially from underfoot, like a display of roman candles, their short strident flight calls like curses of shock at being ejected into the tumult above, their usual jinking escape-flight patterns magnified tenfold as they are propelled like litter across the fields, desperately seeking the certainty of ground again. Despite the violence all around them, gulls hang serenely on barely beating wings, surfing the shore wave where the air hits the shingle ridge, dipping into the eddies and rising on the buffets. Dead trees from distant shores have pushed over the sandbar into the lagoon and now float in the shallows. Fifty shelduck huddle in the lee of the flood embankment, while curlews stand belly-deep in water on the last remaining high spots of marram grass, preferring discomfort to the unpredictability of the tempest. The river and marsh have long ago become one, yet the riverbank is still marked by a narrow dark line of spray-topped waves like a fringing coral reef. The shallow water over the marsh is as calm as an atoll lagoon even though its surface is tarnished by the wind-driven ripples. A male and two female pintails fly strongly, low over the water, composed in flight even in these testing conditions but precision landing in the gusting wind is beyond them and they tumble into the edge of the marsh in a paroxysm of uncoordinated wings and ruffled feathers. Once composure is restored, they become as sublimely slender and elegant on the water as they were in the air, with elongated necks and extended tails as if crafted from wood by the loving hands of a skilled carver; almost caricatures of a duck.

Despite the incitement of the storm, the tide begins to ebb, as ever. Another battle has been fought, the sea has taken some places, new furrows gouged in the mud, and the land has gained others, where sand has settled higher up the beach; the barely perceptible movement of sediment inches remorselessly towards the point, pushing into the river's mouth as it has done for aeons, interrupted just momentarily by the insignificance of the concrete defences. The storm will prove to be the last big one for this winter, not that this has meaning for all. Outside the back door of the house lies the detritus of the wind – in the only sheltered spot it can find is the battered and exhausted form of a razorbill attempting vainly to cling to life, but as its eyes glaze and its life wanes spring is stirring as the wind abates.

What drove you to this place, emaciated wretch?
So lean as to have no more flesh with which to fly,
Wings stripped of blurring beats that kept you in the air
What hardships has the ocean sought to terrify?

Hewn from ferocious cliffs of the Atlantic's edge
To live invisible beyond our land-locked gaze,
From egg confined to perilous rock ledge bare
To adult life upon the ever-rolling waves.

For years your wings have whirred and skimmed the liquid wind
And plunged below the ocean's heaving granite swell
Slipped free between aquamarine and sky so blue
You've seen so many things of which you cannot tell.

Ridden raging storm crests that break with thunderous sound
Passed ships at night on water dappled with moonlight
Flown pelagic wanderings with annual sojourns spent
At cliffs with faithful mate in colonies packed tight

No longer open ocean or the cliffs to dream,
For storm-borne frailty drops you waif limp outside this door
Where huddled from the wind 'twixt corners of this stone
Eyes glaze; storm rider once, now you will ride no more.

APRIL
A HOLE IN THE SKY

Shadows slip silently back into being, still indistinct, their edges fuzzy as light leaks into the eastern sky, diluting the inky blackness to grey and then to paler grey. As the stars fade in the lightening dawn, a barn owl unfolds from a post, enlarging magically, blossoming lily-white and radiant in the remnant dimness. The dusting of lichen-grey and violet on its upperparts, insubstantial like the bloom on sloes, is lost to a flood of golden-amber, its dark eyes depthless, its heart-shaped face impassive. It glides oneiric, low over the tall rank grass touching the air shallowly as if not wishing to disturb its stillness, beating its wings slowly, undulating softly like a gentle pulse on an oscilloscope, a subdued heartbeat of flight. It turns sharply and suddenly; and is gone.

In the rising light, mist slips from its river moorings spilling out of the channel, skirting over the fields on a narrow film of clear air like a hovercraft riding its cushion, swaddling the fields and marsh, swathing the world in intimacy. Sounds are strangely accentuated; the high tide gentle but loud, almost intrusive; the sheep tearing each mouthful of grass from the sward as they graze. Everywhere is wet but not silvered; only a few leaf tips on the brambles carry shining baubles. Indeterminate birds flit across the top of the bushes. Birdsong is largely subdued, but a Cetti's warbler's staccato eruption is repeated between long pauses, loud and clear, for their territories are elongated here, running several hundred metres along the bramble- and reed-edged coast path or the hedges and rhynes around the fields. The curlews passing overhead in the high air are sharp and sunlit while those deploying low along the shore remain dim and obscure. In the east, the topaz-tinged fog eventually expels a silver disc, the sun rising like a full moon, crisp-edged, filtered by the mist, soon becoming too bright to gaze upon. A male blackcap forages unobtrusively in a drying bramble bush. It picks chilled invertebrates from amongst the leaves and thorny stems as it creeps through the twisted branches. A dunnock calls repeatedly, a single high-pitched piercing note irritating in its persistence. A crane-fly rests on a wooden fence, torpid, a film of mist condensed on its outspread legs and wings.

Morning ages in soft monochrome, emerging in stages like a developing photograph, slowly becoming a hand-tinted print; a series of revelations, the mirrored lagoons, the flooded saltmarsh, the overflowing river, and finally the opaque far riverbank, the sunlight sparkling on the water between like a satin brocade. The mist finally clears to reveal cloudless vaulting blue. A rusty shadow drifts across the grass as a fox trots steadily through a field, sending the white scuts of rabbits dashing for cover and woodpigeons clattering into the air. It is confident yet wary, stopping abruptly to listen, ears cocked seeking the direction of a troublesome sound, nose seeking an enticing scent. Reassured it trots onward, disappearing beneath the brambles along the bank of a rhyne. Blue tits search the tips of branches and the underside of leaves fastidiously for food. A chiffchaff gleans invertebrates from a blackthorn bush blossoming in blowzy constellations, flitting lightly amongst the sprays, making occasional sallies to snatch a passing fly. Beyond, gulls and cormorants, many of the latter in heraldic feather-drying pose, congregate on the saltmarsh. Far, far across the river, in the tall oaks surrounding the church tower, the rooks are busy at their rookery, their nests bulky in the still bare branches of the treetops. Like their harsh cawing, lost to the wind before it can ever cross the water, they rarely come over the river to feed. It is as if the river acts as a natural barrier to them, yet the carrion crows that thrive here often fly to its far shore. Fifty redshanks rise from the river's sloping mud banks, flying purposefully across the marsh and fields towards the coast, either heading out to the edge of the ebb tide to feed or commencing the next stage of their northward migration. As they pass low overhead, a constant tittering of contact calls accompanies the blurred rush of their wingbeats.

On the capstone of a tile-roofed barn, a female woodpigeon jumps, a small hop unlike her normal sedate walk. Her semi-circular white neck patches seem to spill from beneath her plain grey hood like a puritan lady's collar beneath her bonnet. Her seductive gait has the male behind produce the same movement, followed by a deep bow with tail fanned to display the dark band at its tip. He raises it high in a slow elegant flowing motion. The female hops again, but when the male bows too close, she flies to a nearby wall, pulling her suitor behind her on an invisible leash of hope, the ritual of courtship. Finally, on a fence post, he mounts her briefly with fluttering wings, mates, and returns to the fence beside her. She steps away, a series of bedraggled hops, and stands motionless as if in some sort of shock, a distance now between them as if coming to terms with the magnitude of the consummation they have just performed, unable now to decide upon how next to proceed. That spell is broken by an interloper, and the male flies across the lane to repel any possible advances towards his mate, then stands guard atop a taller post. The female preens.

She comes low and very fast out of the morning sun with the fresh wind behind her, hugging the sand, her passage marked by a parting bow wave of chestnut-bandoliered shelducks. Far out on the sand spit that grows from the point on an ebb tide, a flock of bar-tailed godwits huddle close, resting on their journey to the immutable northern light, dreaming an idea of the tundra that never really leaves them. Most now bear the deep fiery rufous heads and underparts of breeding plumage. The birds though sleepy are wary, clinging to the furthest reaches of the spit, eschewing land as if it is abhorrent, repelled by its solidity yet not quite aquatic enough to embrace the sea. Now the birds are unnerved. Six hundred pairs of eyes urgently scan the skies. But she's not there. With increasingly powerful beats, muscles rippling, pointed wings flicking rapidly, she charges over the last low rise of the beach and out across the wet sand where a female peregrine keeps pace beneath her, staring up at her from the silvered surface, mirroring her every move. The godwits rise, a salvo of thrashing wings churning the air, panicked calls surging. But the flock is only just airborne and the falcon is at full speed, the gap between the two closing alarmingly quickly. She hurtles towards its centre, cleaving through it, birds parting ahead of her as the sides of raw meat curve away from the blade of a sharp knife, just as she knows they will. In the middle, one bird remains hanging momentarily on the cusp of indecision between left and right, isolated and now the quarry. Darwinian selection or simple happenstance? Isolated it may be but, sleek and athletic, it beats strongly seawards yet is still no match for the peregrine already assailing it. The godwit shuts its wings at the last second, jerks down and right, and ebony talons glint as they skim by. The peregrine overshoots, a gap opens, hope flickers, but she flares her wings, converting speed to height, rolls hard, spinning vertically on her wing tip, and throws herself down once more towards her target, now heading swiftly landward. Once again the godwit jinks and evades. This time the peregrine has anticipated. Half-rolling while completing a half-loop she heads directly back after the godwit. It jinks again, vainly trying to put space between itself and its nemesis. The aerobatics become ever faster, ever tighter, ever more desperate, the peregrine persistent in pursuit. On the fourth pass, feathers fly as talons rake the godwit's straining shoulders. With no choice left, the godwit plunges into the calm grey waters immediately beneath, and for a moment hope again glimmers like an ember in the wind as the falcon, perplexed, flies away. She swivels back. The ember is extinguished. The godwit's fate is sealed. For even as it struggles clear from the water, its wings barely coping with the extra weight of its sodden plumage, the peregrine buries one foot into the flexing muscles. The godwit collapses back into the sea, and the falcon lets go. The godwit flounders, never to find flight again. The peregrine turns one last time, stalls almost to a hover, and plucks the godwit from the water with both feet. She strives to lift her heavy burden, its weak fluttering adding to her difficulties, but as its life ebbs away its weight seems to lighten. The peregrine rises above the water struggling towards the shore, the long legs and bill of her hard-won prey trailing limply behind.

Yet her quest to eat is still not over, her prize only part-won, for any bird carrying potential food is fair game for marauding herring gulls. Four converge quickly around her, making false passes, harrying her in an attempt to get her to drop her prey. Bereft of her aeronautical aplomb, her dogged persistence comes to the fore and although the pursuer is now the pursued, she flies directly, if slowly, shoreward. Hampered by the gulls and the headwind, she finally makes landfall, brushing the dune grass, and disappearing into a hollow to consume her meal.

Deception is afoot in the hedges. The yellow-grey hawthorns are cast with a delicate green haze, their leaf buds loitering on the cusp of opening, hesitant in the face of changeable weather, yet the lengthening days are insistent. The hawthorns have been empty of migrants today; clear overnight skies and calm sunny mornings is prime weather for travel, and all of them have continued north. Early butterflies are abroad. A sulphur-coloured brimstone flies strongly in the dappled coolness of the lane; a peacock, gaudy in maroon with pale blue roundels, flutters nervously between the dandelions' inflated yellow cushions; and an orange-tip flitters over lady's smock at the edge of a meadow, alighting on its pale pink flowers. In the shifting shadows beneath a hedge, a dunnock forages unobtrusively amongst the freshly growing stems of grass and wildflowers. It resembles the detritus of winter, dowdy grey and brindled; a neurotic bird, jerky and exuding timidity. It looks around constantly, flicking leaves aside quickly, snatching at food items as if any time spent away from its paranoid surveillance is time wasted. It pecks and swallows with rapid movements of its mandibles, as if each beakful may be its last.

Intense activity arrests the eye above as a second bird flitters down through the leaves, flicking one wing rapidly, then the other, bouncing animatedly from side to side as it approaches the first bird, now revealed to be a female. She leads him forwards trembling her body gently, and he repeats his display, angling towards her his flicking wing, sometimes flicking both. She ceases hopping and stands very still, bowing forwards and raising her tail high. She fluffs up her feathers and quivers her wings to a blur, wagging her tail back and forth alluringly. The male moves forwards and begins to peck at her cloaca, hesitantly at first, jumping up, down, and around erratically, as if scared of being caught in the act of such intimacy. He becomes bolder as the female continues her ecstatic quivering, sometimes bouncing on her legs as if imploring him to continue. As he does so, her cloaca swells and grows pink, and she starts to make pumping motions with her body, suddenly ejecting a tiny packet of sperm from her previous mating. The male immediately flies at her as if attacking her, and she retreats quickly – but in fact they have made contact and consummated a fleeting union, the male then departing hastily through the branches above. A third bird arrives, also flicking his wings, but this time slowly and more methodically. He flits down to join the female but does not approach closely; he simply follows her every movement, ignorant of his mate's infidelity but probably suspicious of it. He is the alpha male, for this is a polyandrous group. Having accepted the beta male's help to defend his territory, he has to guard his female closely to minimise the chances of the beta male fathering what should be his offspring. But the female is cunning and deliberately promiscuous, for if she can offer the beta male enough chances to believe that he is father to the coming brood, as she has just done, then he will be lured into helping her and the alpha male to raise the brood, something that benefits her whoever the father is. She will repeat the quivering-wing seduction frequently throughout each day, mostly with the alpha male; but therein lies the duplicity, for the beta male may just be the last to mate with her before she lays. Such is the deception to be found in hedges.

Today the swallows returned. Aristotle's perceptive 'One swallow does not a summer make' is as true today as it was over two thousand years ago, for the day is cold and grey with intermittent drizzle and summer still seems far away. Yet it is strange how amongst all the other signs of the changing seasons – the lengthening and warming days, the greening landscape, the spring flowers, the singing birds – that the sight of the year's first swallows is the most palpable indication that summer is coming and sets human hearts briefly aflutter. These four swallows are strangers here. They will not tarry over the fields and hedges of the peninsula, for their summer homes are somewhat northwards still, and the peninsula is just another fleeting vista to add to the many they have already seen. They are silent, so bring none of the companionable chattering of those that will breed around the farmhouse all summer. They skim low over the pastures, their flight direct; yet while their passage is all too brief, they trail a thread of promise behind them in a way that none else do save perhaps the cuckoo.

Where did that swallow dream last night?
What sights,
Slipped silently 'neath fragile wings in flight,
That brought it northward back to these compelling shores?

How did it follow stars so bright?
What insight,
Weaved its path 'neath constellations of the night,
To skim verdant meadows seen just once before?

And while afar in sun at height
Did it delight
In heat and dust; did Africa excite?
Perhaps, yet nuptial lands proved too hard to ignore.

So north past minarets and sights
'Neath moonlight
Silvered like a tempting dream that might
Entice; yet onward to the siren call once more.

And so, where e'er it was last night,
It just might,
Have dreamed of this softer morning light
That dawn brings dancing over England's greener shores.

At three thousand feet over the point, he glided gracefully in the canyons between the dappled buttes of the cumulus. Below, the land ran north along one edge of the bay and west along the other, and in between the silvered blue waters of the channel stretched away, glistening in the spring sunshine, the shadows of the clouds mottling its surface. He closed his wings and fell through a hole in the sky, vertical, revolving slowly in the coruscating brilliance of the warm sunlight, somehow in slow motion like an ash seed corkscrewing from a tree, yet plunging through the well driven between the gleaming turrets of the surrounding clouds, weightless in the speeding air, flickering through the dappled shadows and filtered sunbeams, rhythmically like a car along a tree-lined avenue: mesmeric. He pulled up in the granitic shade below the marmoreal towers, in the cool moats of their foundations still a thousand feet above the ground, flaring upward in a perfect parabola on open wings, feeling the lift rise through his feathers, swimming up through his own vortices like a diver through the bubble trail of his entry through the water. The waders and ducks and pigeons watched from the ground but did not fly, aware of the peregrine's presence yet safe in the knowledge that hysterical flight was unnecessary all the time he was still high and no other peregrine was apparent. He climbed again across the scalloped cloud face through a combination of soaring and powerful wingbeats, the slow efficiency of the thermic lift surpassed by the childlike impatience of wanting to find a way back above the clouds, to find another hole in the sky through which to fall, the rapture of the stoop much too addictive for just one ride.

The bleached reedbeds are awakening. Fresh green stems are just visible above the black oozing depths at the base of last year's wind-tortured growth. The voices lost last summer are rekindling; the first reed warblers, perched low amongst the curving tawny haze of their secret world, seem to act like amplifying vessels, pouring forth the scratching and rustling sounds of the desiccated stems in prolonged harsh exhalations from their pulsating white throats. Above, amongst the nodding empty sepia seed heads, the higher-pitched staccato stuttering of sedge warblers and the more wistful sighs of the black-hooded reed buntings breathe new life through the withered shell of the winter-worn stands.

The warblers have arrived overnight with a change in wind direction, warm southerlies having replaced the cold north-easterly airflow of the past week. In the stunted brambles along the coast path, their newly-emerging leaves tinted bronze around their edges, more migrants are present; whitethroats repeating scratchy refrains, and willow warblers flitting from stem to stem, remaining in one place only momentarily, as if the thorny briars are too hot to grasp. A robin sings from a hawthorn, its song as cool and pure as glacial meltwater. A male linnet perches atop a curving stem, his liquid trilling like an understudy to skylarks. His breast is suffused with rose-pink but his forecrown is not yet crimson. Nearby, his mate holds a beakful of hair and sheep's wool plucked from pieces snagged on the wire fences. She waits, looking around assiduously, then drops into the dark depths of the brambles as if to build. Yet this is just a feint, and she reappears nearby, still holding her precious bundle, before flying a short distance to a new bush, and after continuing to cast about for some moments vanishes into the concealment of the grass and leaves below. The male changes his song to a descending metallic burr, flying up and out over the reedbeds in an ellipse before gliding back to the same perch. The female alights next to him, this time holding a belly feather from a woodpigeon, flashing white like a beacon; the previously tight nest security compromised for a specially coveted furnishing.

Beyond the foreshore, the mud lies empty and expectant like watercolour paper bearing its first umber wash ahead of the artist adding in the detail of the birds. The overwintering waders have long since departed: the northbound passage migrants to the south have still to arrive. Herring gulls drift aimlessly, sculling lightly in leisurely flight through the bright lower air.

Their oceanic laughter rings through the stillness, enlarging it, engulfing it with sound as an incoming tide floods the mudflats. The sky above them is blurred, the high cloud and haze glassy white, the sun bright but directionless. On the riverbank, three immature cormorants stand resting. Brown above and dirty white below, they turn their heads back and forth lugubriously, scanning as if bemused like some form of primordial aquatic life first emerging onto land. Close by, a peregrine is hunkered down on a shingle ridge, at one with the stone. It will be a non-breeding bird, for the wintering pair left some weeks ago for their distant nesting cliffs. Throughout winter, the ebb tide becomes a time of quiet after the activity of the flood – but now, in spring, that restfulness has been supplanted by the constant motion of shelducks displaying and jostling in and around the pools and taking flight, small parties of males chasing individual females. On the short sward of the saltmarsh grass, now vivid with new chlorophyll, a pair of oystercatchers strut and pipe with blood-orange bills held vertically down and just above the surface as they parade together back and forth, cementing their pair bond. The calls are urgent and insistent and penetrating and strangely soulful. Then they too take wing in courtship flight, a slow-flapping motion, the wingbeats curiously delayed so as to resemble the wafting of a pied butterfly, borne on a current of liquid calls.

Light cloud brushes the early morning sky. The air is calm, the sea is flat, blue rises inexorably on a spring tide. Whimbrels titter hesitantly along the coast. Swallows stream steadily across the fields, addicted to the flight that pulls them on to the narcotic of the north. Amongst them are small groups of late sand martins, along with the first white rump of a house martin. In the lane, a rabbit lollops away, its white tail bouncing after it and a baby scampering behind that. On either side, the witches' hedges grow twisted and tangled, tormented and blasted by the wind, burnt by the storm-borne sea salt, sculpted into survival shapes. They are suffused with the green of bursting buds, but there will be no room here for the delicate interlacing of leaves found in a sheltered forest that maximises the surface for efficient photosynthetic production, just whatever can emerge in the face of the ever-belligerent elements. They resound to the tinkling of linnets.

A whitethroat rises briefly from the deep shade of the brambles to deliver its scratchy warble, then withdraws, darting down through the thorn-armoured stems, only to ascend moments later and reprise it from a new perch. It flies lightly away across a gap into the safety of another bush, and looks back as if enticing one to follow. It is difficult to comprehend how such frailty and timidity can make the trip to sub-Saharan Africa and back each year. Blackthorn bushes are in full flower, a pearly opacity of softness concealing the sharp black thorns within. Their heady scent is lighter and sweeter and less pungent than that of the hawthorns still to come. The flowers seem showier, too, but perhaps only because their leaves are not yet out, while the hawthorns' flowers open amongst their leaves and hence seem a little more decorous. A willow warbler sings softly while foraging aptly in a mature willow, its hormones ahead of its journey's progress to its woodland breeding site. The bubbling beginning is followed by cascading slippery glissandos, silvery like water, redolent of sleepy slow-flowing streams and sun-flecked pools.

In the same pasture, seven wheatears feed amongst the cowslips which dip their nodding yellow trumpets as if sipping the dew. The birds are in crisp plumage, icy blue-grey upperparts with black wings and warm tawny underparts, the males with black masks, all with white rumps that flash in flight as they flit from molehill to tussock to ruined wall, always favouring a high point. Their visit is transitory, for they were not here an hour ago and their journey is as yet unfinished. But for two other birds, their journey is. From the quiet northward trickle of swallows overhead, one bird dips, to be joined a moment later by another. And that small movement, described by that small word, is the difference, for it marks the completion of their long journey. They land beside each other on the roof of a barn. The first of the swallows that breed here have returned home. They again take wing, but their flight has now lost that purposeful urgency of travel and instead assumed the relaxed unhurriedness of arrival; curving around back and forth, looping in and out of the barn, skimming low to sip from the pond, then out over the fields to feed over the pasture, apprising themselves of the area like owners opening up a summer holiday home, checking the familiar, alert to signs of change.

While the migrants are still travelling or just arriving, those birds that have survived winter here are already raising their young. A female blackbird, holding two worms in her dusky yellow beak, struggles to extricate a third from between the wet grass stems, tugging it carefully with legs braced forwards, pausing when the worm constricts to thicken and grip the sides of its burrow, then tugging again quickly when it relaxes, pulling another length free, playing it like an angler does a weighty catch, gradually hauling it free of its burrow. She drops the other two on the grass and jabs at her new prize, pecking at it to stun it, then laying it with the other two, folding each, and picking all up in a single package. With the looped worms dangling and wriggling gently from the sides of her beak, she flies to her cupped nest hidden in the bushes nearby to deliver another meal to her insatiably hungry nestlings.

The tide stills. The water is flat and lifeless, the surface sullied only by the softest of breezes casting it with a non-reflecting sheen like brushed aluminium; the sky grey under lightly creased stratus, yet bright and slightly glaring. A polar bite remains insinuated into the light easterly breeze. Seven metres of water have compressed the land into a narrow sliver, the point and the saltmarsh unrecognisable, brimming with rising water, brimming with rising light. The sonorous yelps of a great black-backed gull reverberate over the wide expanse of the river, like distant cries for help. A few teal dabble amongst the dead grasses and organic debris that have floated to the surface on the tide. Four dozen carrion crows feed along the river's edge like scavengers ahead of an African bush fire, picking at items displaced by the extraordinarily high waters. The numbers of crows belie the old countryside lore that 'a crow in a crowd is a rook, a rook on its own is a crow'. There are constant altercations over morsels, the birds scuttling and squabbling with flailing wings and stabbing beaks. Having taken a wrong bearing and been caught out by the tide, a hare, wet and bedraggled and cold, lopes miserably along a path, stopping often to shiver warmth back into its muscles. Still disoriented, it turns and lollops through the grass, disappearing over a bank to where yet more water and misery awaits it.

Grey has become greyer. Drizzle now falls in waves across the fields, soaking feathers and fur alike. Snails are active in large numbers, inching forwards over the filmed grass and cut-leaved cranesbill. Woodpigeons mope on fence posts, raising their heads impassively to watch a vixen walking slowly through the cowslips below. The static shape of one moves and stretches, first with a bow and flexing of both wings, then each leg and wing extended to one side; then a shake of the tail, a ninety-degree turn on the fence post to change the view, and it returns to a motionless sculpted form for another hour. The drizzle becomes rain, dropping the last of the blackthorn blossom from the bushes, the petals discarded like a lace veil rumpled in the wet grass below, leaving the styles and stamens shrivelled and pinky-brown, the tiny green ova now set and beginning their six-month growth into deep blue sloes. The shower drops more than petals, for out of the wet morning sky falls a field-full of migrants, wheatears and whinchats, their journey interrupted by the decreasing visibility. They feed on the short turf while another bird, a female common redstart, flirts from a fence post, trembling her orange tail discreetly while looking back over her wing coquettishly. Twenty minutes later, when the shower ceases, all depart, climbing together into the north, a fragile flock of tiny wings with so many miles still to travel. Birdsong swells as the watery sun strengthens. Skylarks dance puppet-like, climbing silver strings of song high into the sky; a wren trills with gusto from brambles along a rhyne; a blackbird provides a virtuoso coloratura in its fluting falsetto from the top of a willow. Woodpigeons are active again, the males displaying between their bouts of accented rhythmic purring. They flap frantically, climbing steeply out over the fields, then spread their wings and fan their tails, wallowing upwards, belly-flopping over into a stall, capsizing forwards and sideways, gliding down on outstretched wings, sometimes repeating the manoeuvre before arcing gracefully down towards a perch back in the hedgerows.

Two hours after high tide, and the mud is reappearing. A flight of forty dunlin, all in black-bellied breeding plumage, skim low across the shore, espousing feeding grounds in order to make progress across the shrinking river's mouth, there to turn north once more along its far shore. Two of the crows are now on the foreshore, insistent and belligerent as ever, bullying a flock of forty migrant oystercatchers into the air to feed on their patch of mud, as if the rest of the empty beach is not enough. A line of migrant curlews ripple over the sea. The lost souls of their melancholy whistles have become ghosts of the departed winter, their calls now thinner and longer, accelerating strings of rising tremulous bubbles presaging summer on the open moors of the north.

MAY
A FILIGREE OF MUSIC

May day morning, viridian and fecund and humid. The latest grey shower-cloud leaks fine raindrops, sending tiny ripples interlacing across the surface of the pond. From the green aurora, deep in the willows, the thick air palpitates with the subdued sweet warble of a blackcap's sub-song, a restrained refrain of treble bubbles that trembles in the aromatic light beneath the translucent leaves. No territorial declaration this, simply the response to overflowing hormones in a traveller uncommon this far out on the peninsula, yet numerous close upstream. But this is merely a rehearsal, like an orchestra warming up before the main performance or a painting viewed in shadow before complete exhibition. For suddenly he delivers the full rhapsody with fluttering throat, louder, purer, more fluid, the notes cavorting within the sun-sifted auditorium beneath the canopy, mesmerising liquid bursts of song interspersed with momentary pauses, the notes tumbling over themselves to leave the rich pinkness of his open gape and frolic fleetingly in the dancing shadows. For two full minutes he sings, his whole tiny body swollen with song, shuddering with sound, heaving with effort. Yet effortless the notes sparkle, the phrases frothing with vibrancy; for two full minutes the listener's ears lift the heart in passion. Then, as if a cork is returned to a bottle, the sub-song is reprised and he falls silent to search for food; a passing minstrel, gone tomorrow.

Nearby, swallows perch on wires or sweep from daylight into the hooded shadows of the barn, their soft-edged twitterings bouncing off the brick walls and flagstone floor like hurried intimate conversations. Above, stock doves display from the roof in circuits out over the fields while a collared dove on the weathervane croons hollowly and ever-so-slightly hoarsely. A haze of blackbird song shimmers in the air, the warmth from their syrinxes held within their tremulous notes. Over the buttercup-gilded meadows, a skylark climbs in a diminishing circle, an ascending spiral, a rising vortex, until far, far above, it becomes stationary, a mere dot that the eye strains to locate in the blue between the swirling vapour of the shower-clouds. With wings ablur, tail fanned, and beak open, it heralds the unfolding morning with a chord of jewels discarded with philanthropic abandon. Rich beyond imaginings, it casts its wealth of silvered euphonies to the celestial winds, to fall to whatever ear may catch them, a filigree of music glittering earthwards, sprinkling the fields with shimmering song. Then as wingbeats cease, it changes tempo, and on open wings parachutes lightly earthwards, turning slowly like a falling sycamore seed before a final plunge to a clod of soil – and silence. And all around the rain begins to softly fall once more.

One mild evening as the sun is sinking and the light fading, a bar-tailed godwit spreads its wings and lifts its toes from the mud, to be followed by another and another and another, until the remainder of the flock lifts as one. They circle once, low, allowing the stragglers to coalesce, the brick-red plumage of some glowing in the last rays of sun, then together spiral higher before stretching out into a line and setting a course to the north. The birds, refuelled from a day or two of intensive feeding in the bay and now laden with fat deposits, ascend slowly and heavily with wings flexing and muscles straining, gradually leaving the glistening mud behind, nacreous in the gloaming. The flock climbs steadily up through the canyons between the cumulus clouds, now lavender-grey and dimming as the line of day moves west – darkness already fallen below on the mudflats they have just left; up through the last of the light and into the dark where a hundred thousand stars reside, feeling their way through the twilight, guided by a sense that we do not possess and powered only by beating hearts. They are swapping one edge for another: the edge of the tideline for the edge of endurance, seeking the land of eternal light, for the high Arctic calls and the urge to go home is second only to the urge to survive. Are adrenalin levels high? Does anxiety flow in their veins as their wings build into a steady rhythm? The sad smile of nostalgia and the bright hope of the future are probably beyond their conceptual horizons, yet do they feel trepidation or confidence, or are those just human concepts, a result of greater cognitive powers? Or are their smaller brains fully engaged with navigating? Possibly either, since what reasoning creature would hurl itself into the skies on a migration of thousands of miles if it truly understood the perils ahead of it?

Northwards, then, for one day or two or three depending on course and destination and the will of the winds, north-west to Iceland and Greenland, north-east to Lapland and Svalbard or Arctic Russia, continuing the long flight to summer, there to swap one edge for yet another, this time the edges of the northern landmasses, the permafrost pools of the thawing tundra. We may understand their lives, their journeys from the mudflats at the end of sinuous rivers snaking to the sea in tropical West Africa; their stopovers where the Sahara meets the open ocean in Mauritania; more stopovers in the coastal wetlands of continental Europe and here in England; their breeding ranges in the Arctic. We know their breeding ecology, their patterns of moult, we know their energetics, we have even deciphered the cues they use for navigation; we marvel that individuals of the same species who live around the Pacific rim can cross twelve thousand kilometres of ocean from Alaska to New Zealand in eleven days and nights of non-stop flying; all this … and yet we will never get close to understanding what life on the edge is really like.

In the first hesitant dimness, a blackbird's fluting whistles lance the dawn, the notes ascending like a whale's voice rising through the thickness of the ocean, shimmering at the edges with vibrancy. Morning breaks like a recalcitrant daughter dressed in emerald finery, decorated with lace and pearls, yet sulky under dark grey skies. The buttercups and daisies in the meadows remain folded in the dull light. The land has forgotten the sea that has retreated far into the channel, forgotten its quiet susurration and its louder roaring, forgotten its motion; all is silent and still. A reed bunting sings its sweet song, somehow redolent of a time when England was less populated, more rural, a slower and quieter place. Shadows shorten as the sun rises and the waking grass stirs and eddies, brushed by the first fingers of a breeze. Willow seeds drift upwards on the warming morning air like heaven-bound angels. Sheep are ragged, their fleeces shedding in chunks ahead of shearing, but the lambs remain neat and woolly. They are large and stocky now, buxom around the loins, no longer able to jump and skip, but slowly taking on their mothers' lethargy, although running games sometimes still find attraction. From somewhere on the mudflats a herring gull laughs as if at a joke the rest of the world has missed: the slow ringing elation of triumph, a taunting proclamation of being, once the essence of the coast but now a sound so familiar to many urban locations that it seems somehow discrepant in a setting without buildings. A little egret comes to land in the shallows of a pool, yellow feet pattering the surface of the water, dark legs stumbling as they find the unseen mud below the surface and absorb the residual forward momentum of the flight, like a person caught off-balance at the end of an escalator.

The breeze has become fresher, the wind rising rapidly now, the sky changing, glacial clouds growing, overblown like wedding cakes. The air was warm but the strong north-westerly has become chilly, a sharpness more akin to early autumn than to the culminating days of spring. Cattle sit in the lee of hedges reminiscent of sullen children huddled behind windbreaks on an English holiday beach. A crow flaps heavily over the drying lagoon, rocking slightly while navigating the gusts, when out of the saltmarsh a pied missile launches skywards following the orange tracer of its bill. Silently but violently it intercepts the startled crow, the two switchbacking together through the sky, the oystercatcher now piping shrilly. The crow, normally the harrier, is surprised by the turned tables and vehemence of the onslaught, and makes no effort to do anything but flee. With the perceived threat negated, the oystercatcher breaks off its attack and glides gently back down to the saltmarsh to resume guard near its mate, sitting on their eggs on a shingle island nearby.

A little egret flaps out towards the sea. Finding progress difficult in the burgeoning wind, it desists and turns, and makes rapid progress back across the saltmarsh without further need for flapping. A small flock of dunlin skitters across the wet sand, just the faintest of frayed black staining their bellies. Their dreams of the uplands or the high Arctic have been doused by weeks of strong headwinds delaying northward flight. They rise rapidly from the sand, responding reflexively to the shape of a falcon, but return on recognising the smaller shape and flatter wingbeats as a kestrel and therefore of little threat to them.

Late morning and the landscape is strangely glaucous, the leaves on the trees and bushes inverted silver by the wind. All around is now in motion, sienna reed-heads bobbing on their tawny stems; a grey sea, running high and topped with muddied horses rushing shoreward; sunspots careening across it turning the dark grey to pale ochre and back; gulls riding the rollercoaster of the gusts with equanimity. Swallows feed low, slaloming over the swaying grass, dipping into the sward like shearwaters between waves of the sea, taking insects disturbed from the tops of the stems. Only the kestrel's head remains still, wings flickering alternately slow or fast, a reflex reaction to maintain his geostationary position. He drops slightly, flapping lightly away, dismissive of the strengthening wind, then turns and pulls up into another hover which he holds momentarily before dropping vertically twenty feet and hovering again, a sure sign of possible prey. He breaks hover once again, this time diving vertically, russet wings flicked back and upwards, pale grey tail narrowed and raised. With yellow legs fully extended, he plunges into the green softness of the grass below, remains but moments, and rises already in level flight clutching the dark rounded shape of a limp small mammal in his grip. He flies heavily to the shingle ridge of the riverbank, landing on driftwood to consume his meal, but is instantly disturbed by the perennial paranoia of the oystercatchers. Once again he takes to the air to avoid their dive-bombing and, with his prey now clutched tightly to his belly and his mind changed, sets off across the fields and hedges on the half-mile journey to his mate incubating on a nest in one of the farm buildings in the village.

The luxuriant bushes and trees are rocking now, bucking and wallowing like heavily laden ships in high seas. With the trees and hedges in full leaf, this will be a shaping storm. It is a misconception that the curving hedges and stunted trees grow that way because of the constant winds, particularly those in winter. This is not so, for in winter they are dormant, unresponsive to all but the most violent squalls that may snap twigs and branches, pruning at random. Instead the trees and hedges are sculpted by the irregular late-spring and summer storms which deposit salt ripped from the wave crests onto their growing windward leaves. There it will desiccate the turgid cells by osmosis, shrivelling and deforming them so that in the days to come those leaves will scorch rust-coloured then curl and fall as if they have been fire-damaged, or will wilt and blacken as if corrupted by disease, while those in the lee continue to grow green; a natural pruning that moulds that woody vegetation into survival shapes, sloping gently away from the windward side but sharply vertical on the lee side like an escarpment, or slimmed and bent into aerodynamic shapes akin to the tails of witches' brooms.

Cumulus crown the eastern hills like far distant vistas of snow-capped sierras. The sea breeze is increased by high tide bringing cooler water close to the shore. It ruffles the grass, bending the trees and bushes, and makes the sea a restless and vocal partner. Its chill edge removes any comfort from the evening's soft spring sunshine. Small birds find it troublesome, descending from exposed branches and swaying stems into the base of brambles and reeds. Song has largely been silenced. Only the irrepressible chatter and scraping of the reed warblers remains, yet even this is subdued. The big tides of late spring and summer are not high enough to flood the saltmarsh; instead the river lies like a blue lake corralled between its lush green banks, the lagoons parched and dusty, crazed like old glazed pottery, and empty of birds save the swallows sweeping overhead. Shelduck chases are short now, the birds preferring to snooze, head under wing, on the short grass. Gulls stand, seemingly bored.

A vixen saunters from a hedge and sits on her haunches in the shelter of its lee where the dense brambles meet the hay meadow. Sleek and rufous, she soaks up the evening rays, her lower muzzle, throat and foreneck white and shaggy, her pointed ears and nose coal-black. She is not alone for long. A small cub appears, its fur grey and soft, its pale blue-grey eyes set in a face still rounded by youth. It sits beside her, unconsciously adopting her pose in miniature but gazing up at her imploringly as if to ask 'What do we do now we are here?' As if in answer, three siblings knock it over as they charge out from the earth where they were born, excavated in the sandy ground and concealed far back under the bushes. They stop and look around, staring blankly with a lack of perception at things distant, their shiny eyes still unfocused. Close to, they recognise their mother and each other, and their boisterous confusion begins again: podgy little bodies with short tails and rounded muzzles chasing through the edge of the buttercups, falling over and being pounced upon as they roll around in the grass, their movements clumsy and poorly coordnated, their soft black paws large and loose on the end of short unsteady legs. Slowly their enthusiasm wanes, and their mother becomes a more interesting distraction. First a game of muzzle to muzzle, then climbing on her back, then biting her ear; the vixen absorbs all with everlasting maternal patience while maintaining constant vigilance, her ears twitching, her penetrating gaze roving and distant but unconcerned. Eventually she rises and walks out along the top of the low ridge that marks the ancient dune line, the coast long since advanced seawards, and there, where the grass grows shorter, she calls softly to the cubs, who stumble after her to suckle in the evening sunshine bathing all in its soft rich light.

The distant snowcaps are thawing, the sierras eroding into rounded tors, geological time hastened from aeons to hours as the warm updraughts cool and decay. In the west, the sea rises to meet the sun which has slipped behind fragments of low cloud, casting all prematurely into the cool shadow of night. As the light begins to fade and the breeze dies away, the blackbirds' fragile flutings float from the tops of willows into stilling air. The first dampness rises on the grass and the buttercups, now tightly folded in the meadows. Kiss-curls of cirrus feather the heavens, writing change across the evening sky, frayed edges turning coral-pink like flamingo plumes floating in a pool of blue.

As the first photons push into the curved edge of the dark void of the earth's shadow, an avian muezzin calls, but not the faithful to their prayers, rather celebrating the return of the life-giving sunlight in the east. More prosaically, he sings a statement of presence – I am alive and still here; for the landless dwellers of the underworld circle each morning, seeking gaps that nocturnal deaths have brought, in which they can advance their own territorial claims. For despite the romanticised poetry and prose written about the dawn chorus, it is believed to be merely a proclamation of ownership of that most basic requirement for breeding – a territory. Whether sprawling over a large range or confined to a single flowering bush, whether defended all year or for just a few weeks, that need to secure a space for itself amongst others of its kind to fulfil the first two laws of all life – to survive and reproduce – is all-consuming. And advertising is key – sight, sound, smell – all elemental in repelling neighbours' incursions and, just as important, holding at bay those individuals within the surplus population who have not yet been able to find their space in which to breed, for they are too young, too weak, too sick: the oppressed, the have-nots. Yet not all the owners survive each night, and first light brings a surge of hope and the best opportunities for the have-nots to have. And hence the owners sing.

> He wakes to find he
> Is a being and as a being
> Sings to show he is.

Fine drizzle falls from low fragmented cloud. It casts a stillness across the morning fields, the air stirred only slightly by fragments of breeze. The horizon is a faded pencil sketch, details reduced to monochrome outlines and misty shapes. Inactivity pervades. Pigeons and buzzards and crows hunch on bushes and posts as if waiting for the wet to relent, a mould of fine silver droplets growing on their mantles. Even the swallows seem sluggish. Only the sparrows and blackbirds are busy, their feathers dark and slicked from their continued movement as they dutifully collect and carry food for their nestlings. In the spongiform silence only one sound rings across the fields, the insistent familiarity of the cuckoo's binary onomatopoeia. It leaps from distance and bounces from proximity, hard to pin down as the bird moves invisibly amongst the flowering bushes. The heavy fragrance of hawthorn blossom eddies in the air. The scent, loosened by the damp, is heady and thickly sweet yet imbued with an edge of earthy sourness. It envelopes the hollows over the rhynes with a cloying hallucinogenic aura like an eiderdown of scent. The tight clusters of blossoms are still blushed pink with newness, a tint they will soon lose as they age and spread white across whole bushes. Less opulent than the blackthorn that preceded it a few weeks previously, it is more sugar-frosting than champagne froth. The elder bushes are also in full bloom now. The heads of tiny five-pointed white stars are dusted with cream stamens in flat-topped corymbs, like a floral replica of the Roger Dean fantasies adorning the cover of *Yessongs*. A sudden flapping from the centre of one bush reveals a young great tit. Short-tailed, big-headed, and wide-eyed, it raises its sooty crown above its cream cheeks and yellow gape – startled. It looks all around, head moving quickly, torn between the difficulties of new flight and the urge to flee, the anxiety threatening to tear it apart. It collapses clumsily back into the cover of the brambles. Through a gap in the clouds sunshine spills across the fields and immediately, as if in response, a woodpigeon purrs. The drizzle falters.

Spring song returns. A sedge warbler rasps from a low bramble stem at the edge of the reedbed. Strident, it is a flood of high-pitched ratcheting and low-pitched churring, underlain with an agitated fretfulness and interspersed with a medley of phrases stolen from other species plaited into a seamless braid of sound; a chaotic conversation of birdsong lasting minutes that leaps and lurches from a single bright orange gape – scolding alarms of a blackbird, the tail-end trills of a wren, the piping of distant oystercatchers, a great tit's ringing repetitions, the sweet seeping of a reed bunting, and the harsh metallic spike of a swallow's alarm note.

Then abruptly, silence; a pause of a few seconds, followed by a hesitant rebeginning before he launches full speed into a new song stream this time with a different medley of mimicry – a robin's cascade, a yellow wagtail's soft whistle, a blue tit's chatter, even the soft tittering copied from a passing whimbrel. The more mimicry he can include the more desirable he becomes to a female. His song is an aural peacock's tail. Occasionally he rises from the reeds on slow-beating, floaty wings, arcing to an apex at the full crescendo of his song then tilting over to glide a steep scarp slope back into the tawny stems. Deeper into the bed, reed warblers rattle their more diffident but more incessant chatter, sometimes frenetic, sometimes slow, sometimes single notes with pauses between but never long enough to be a silence, somehow repetitive yet always different, ever nervous, with no defined end or beginning, just a near endless cascade. It rises and falls like rasping breaths, like the very soul of the reedbed itself. Occasionally they too ascend optimistically on song flights to explore the world beyond the confines of their vertical horizons but quickly sink back again, the vaulting blue abode of the skylarks above an ambition too far.

Morning bubbles with the hollow resonance of a cuckoo; its buoyant ringing call the quintessential sound of an early English summer. Yet for some it is but a fading memory, for others a sound they have never heard in the wild, as the inexorable decline in the numbers returning each year strips another layer of character from the core of the commonplace. Here, for now, it still ferments the sweetness of early summer. Overnight rain has left the ground damp and richly coloured, the air cool. Newly-emerged small coppers and common blues flutter through the yellow haze of buttercups and trefoils. In the dark universe of a dewpond, a galaxy of white water-crowfoot flowers garlands the surface. Steel-coloured whirligig beetles whizz around them in endless chases; the patterns of spring territoriality are repeated at every level. A great crested newt floats amongst them like a black and leathery water dragon with a spotted fiery belly and a set of yellow toes that any pedicurist would covet. Overhead, skylarks abseil down the final notes of their arias as they descend from the apex of their song flights, while whitethroats set forth skywards seemingly in hope of emulating them but, in realising that futility, fall sharply back to bramble tops where their discordant songs remind them, like students, of the practice still needed for musical perfection; practice that never seems to get beyond the first few phrases. Goldfinches tinkle pleasingly. The first swifts of the year have arrived on lambent wings, slanting north towards the point.

That line of clouds, originally no more than a fleeting thought on the distant horizon, now burgeons on the consciousness as it darkens the sky. The light cosseting breeze has gone. The urgency of the downdraught, the harbinger of storm, now whips through the air. Song has ended, birds have vanished. Rain starts to fall in stinging sheets. Cows turn their backs. The sea writhes and churns the mud in chaotic swell. Yet there, suddenly, surfing the front of the squall, oblivious to its violence, not one but maybe three hundred Manx shearwaters, gliding over the waves with never a wingbeat to miss. A choreographed ballet of effortless interweaving movement, wings taut, angled slightly back and down towards the tips, the birds tilting gently black above then white below as they catch just the right amount of updraught off the waves, first right to rise then left to fall slanting over the rollers, caressing and teasing the horses just below that would pull them to their doom if only they could reach. Mercurial as it came, the carnival is but fleeting, now over here but moving on up the funnel of the channel, its surfers travelling ahead of it leaving only smiles behind. When the winds and squalls abate, they will drift back unseen in midstream, returning to the open sea and their nocturnal islands. As the sun reappears, the whitethroats resume their music practice.

The smell of warmth rises from the track into the cool green sheltered hollow of the lane. Two speckled woods, fresh from their overwintering chrysalises, pirouette a helical ballet in a brume of pheromones, spiralling up through the emerald shade and parting company in the bright light streaming above. The sun shines; contentment courses through skin and feather. It is early summer sun, not yet burning, its heat dissipated through a gauze of high cloud that subdues the shadows and softens the light; a luxuriant warmth to be welcomed after days chilled by wind and grey cloud. The hayfields are a palette of colour, echoes of times long past; swathes of buttercups and yellow rattle, clusters of aromatic white cow parsley, foci of purple vetch, pink restharrow and cranesbills, pinpricks of white mouse-ear and yellow black-medick, dark club-heads of ribwort plantain. Bumble bees ponder over red clover. Common blue butterflies fuss on white-fringed wings around cushions of bird's-foot trefoil. Swallows skim the hazy panicles of bents and bromes, meadow-grass and soft-grass, crested dog's-tail, timothy, and fescues that are surging into the sunlight above their leaves, soon to be seeking the wind to lavish their pollen far and wide. In the absence of oak trees on the peninsula a great tit gleans caterpillars from the brambles, carrying each one individually to its nest in a hole in a distant stone wall. Dextrous and intelligent as the species is, it appears quirky that these birds have failed to master the skill of catching and carrying multiple prey. Nearby, the stems of another bush tremble softly in time to a repetitive, descending, attenuated rattle. The dry little song betrays the presence of a lesser whitethroat, sunspots playing across its plain plumage as it flits insubstantially through the yellow freshness of the flourishing canopy. The leaves shudder and the bird flits up, now holding a pale green caterpillar in the forceps of its beak, its white outer tail feathers flicking in agitation in time with a quiet call like two stones tapped gently together. As it approaches its nest deep in the dusty brown shadows and thorns below, its mate rises and wipes a white faecal sac from its newly-hatched nestlings on a twig. Parental duties are now all-consuming.

Sea radish is in bloom along the shingle at the edge of the coastal brambles. Superficially like rapeseed, it is an anarchic plant, tap-rooted like an elongated parsnip to provide solid purchase amongst the shifting stones. Above ground it is tall and wild and unkempt, grasping space with coarse twisting spreading branches, an aerosol of pale yellow flowers misting their tips that in time will give rise to its gnarled and pointed fleshy seedpods whose peppery taste bestows its name. It is avoided by bees but beloved by small and green-veined whites and orange-tips. The hawthorn blossom is coming to its end as the month that bears its country name closes, the pink blush in the white petals long gone, now infused only in the tiny anthers. On some flowers, the white petals are withering, crisp and brown around their edges prior to their fall, the fruits set on their journey to crimson haws. On one of these ovaries, a tiny weevil, dull metallic turquoise as if encased in copper oxide armour, searches for its microscopic food.

Beyond the reeds the sea is flat, an abstract of opaque white calm and brown-grey patches where pockets of wind catch and ripple its surface. The distance is invisible, dissolved in a glassy haze. Ten curlews inhabit the shimmer at the edge of a fragile line of thick and oily waves noiselessly caressing the shore. Non-breeders, they have rejected the lure of the uplands to pass an unproductive but leisurely summer on the mudflats. At the point, gulls loaf in idleness. Shelduck sleep on the sand or nuzzle the freshly exposed mud with their scarlet bills, browsing the tiny saltwater snails that in turn graze the algae that grows as a film in the interstitial spaces of the sediment. A sandwich tern drifts by, a bird of the oceans and beaches. While it is commoner and earlier further west, here

157

it is the last of the migrants seeking a summer home. Its flight is light and fluent, powered by deep leisurely beats of its sleek and elongated narrow wings. It follows the yellow tip of its black bill. A female oystercatcher rises from three mottled eggs on a tiny island and parades silently with her mate, walking in parallel with bills pointed at the ground. A brief quiet display of reaffirmation to break the boredom of incubation before she turns and sits, folding her pink legs beneath her, shuffling to settle her brood patch comfortably back over the eggs. He picks tiny stones from the ground, flicking some away with abandon while placing others carefully closer towards the nest with no obvious objective, perhaps a simple displacement activity. A cuckoo's call drifts listlessly across the river from far away on the distant bank. Apart from the simplicity that makes its recognition so easy, perhaps another reason for its familiarity is that it probably carries further than any other bird's call. Despite the demands of the breeding season, an easy peace floats lightly across the peninsula, basking in the comfortable warmth, decorated by the abundance of flowers, luxuriating in their fragrances, and serenaded by the birds' soft songs. A week before the meteorological end of spring, summer has settled into place.

JUNE
MONSTERS ON THE STAIRS

Three minutes past four, the sun still lost below the eastern horizon, yet a pale suffusion slowly trespasses into the sanctity of night, flooding the humid cloudy dawn like an incoming tide. In this first, almost imperceptible light, an invisible piper pierces the last vestiges of the night's silence with a single hesitant immaculate note that punctures the silken stillness like a blade splitting night from day. The blackbird heralds the aurora with pure phrases trembling in the warm moist air; phosphorescent music, bright and shimmering, thermal notes ever rising until so distant from their source they simply merge with the slightest breeze, a voluptuous fluting cascade of liquid whistles that courses to the soul like the warmth of sunshine penetrating skin. Swallows' songs provide a choral harmony ahead of flights to greet the blushing sky: urgent streams of oddly angular twitterings, not quite harsh, their edges rounded as if eroded and softened, yet still carrying a core density of sound. As the red rim in the east consumes the dark ahead of it like the glowing embers of burning paper, Brownian motion dissolves the greyness into the spectral solvent of the morning, colour imperceptibly permeating the fading grey. The blackbird, having led the first movement, has fallen silent; the swallows have taken wing.

The earliest rays of the rising sun ignite that Spartacus moment, when suddenly one bird's song gives way to a chorus of others, all announcing their identity together; the rollicking bombast of wrens, the rippling cascade of robins, the repetitive interjections of great tits, the faltering warbles of dunnocks, the cadenced chanting of greenfinches. Starlings jabber, house sparrows chirrup manically, whitethroats scratch out of key, reed warblers grate from the fringes of reeds. In the damp cover below them, a moorhen croaks – a short guttural frog-like utterance introducing the next performers upon the dawn stage. Throaty breathy cooing from a woodpigeon floats sultry in the heavy air, the aural equivalent of smoke rings, briefly having form before dispelling into the amorphous stillness of the morn. A goldfinch tinkles from overhead, a handful of diamonds thrown into the pale velvet of the dawn's soundscape. From across the fields, a coarse shout from an uncouth carrion crow irritates and announces raucous bravado from more crows as they happen upon a roosting sparrowhawk and begin the incessant torment of the day. The sonorous lethargy of the woodpigeon changes as the performer responds to a distant rival across the village, so its cooing accelerates, pumping through the air with steroid-like enhancement, the nearby air seeming to bulge from the pressure. In the meadow, a dog fox saunters through the long grass on a path it made months ago and uses often. Lithe and grizzled, it is the product of genetic happenstance as much as passing time, and its lower fur is slicked with dew. With its head hung low and ears sleeked back, its front mirrors its slightly curved pointed tail, giving symmetry to front and rear. It pauses momentarily to sniff the air, then trots on purposefully, another night's hunting over.

Summer dawn when the air is chill and light is inchoate
That instant when no colour lives; the world is learning greys
That moment when the wind is lost and silence emanates
On an unmarked stage in stillness, Aurora's piper plays

Where not-quite-night meets not-quite-morn, but in the gap between
The shining music flaunts itself, cavorting, dancing free
Not to the eye still struggling, confused with shapes half seen
But in the stillness clarion, to ear a tracery

Unseen the trembling throat pours forth the molten mellow strain
A stream of melodic arias each quaver rising true
Rich like a well-aged chardonnay, yet bubbling like champagne
The notes gleam bright in the silence, like sunbeams off the dew

The fluting glitters in the chill and floats across the field
Dawn's beautiful soliloquy, joined by the crows' harsh caw
Morning breaks, now colour's born, the songster is revealed
Black-garbed, gold-billed, and all alone; yet soloist no more.

The afternoon breeze has dropped. Warm air begins to chill. The damp smell of evening rises. In verdant fields, cows sit in anticipation of old wives' rain, or perhaps rumination is simply more comfortable sprawled in soft summer grass. Around them the airy calls of a cuckoo rebound in the still air like little pockets of drowsy warmth, a joyous childlike familiarity to them. It flies from the top of a hawthorn, changing song posts. Falcon-like in shape, its flight is delicate and buoyant, yet somehow less assured than a falcon's, with more hurried shallower wingbeats and tail loosely fanned. It almost exudes a nervousness as to whether it can stay airborne. Then minutes later, from far away, its call hollows once again across the evening fields. A pulse of fear clatters woodpigeons from the grass, startling a female roe deer. She stands frozen against the hawthorn bushes that the cuckoo left, coat dark and slick, ears erect, nose twitching, instinctively aware of danger but unable quite to discern its shape, for no noise or smell reaches her straining senses: she holds, motionless, bristling with inner conflict – to run and waste energy in fleeing from unreal danger, or to hold and fall prey to a particularly clever predator? She rocks hesitantly as tension rises within her until it becomes unbearable and she bounds away over the moist grass. Away from what she does not know, just away is good enough. Nearby, a hare has folded itself into the grass, just ears, eyes, and nose visible above the grass, like an English hippopotamus. A vixen appears from below a nearby hedge, and as she does the hare pulls further downwards, hugging the ground, submerging like a submarine into a green and yellow ocean.

Skylarks sing from high above, silvered rivulets of cascading incandescence. Closer to, a robin's song sparkles in the evening air like dew in sunlight, a multi-faceted yet insubstantial bauble of sound suspended, glowing momentarily, vibrating in the stillness, replaced by another and then another as the robin stakes a claim to its space in the firmament. As the pink flush ebbs from the west, a male blackbird sings evensong from the highest perch available to it, its golden bill turned heavenwards, sending an endless series of ringing rhymes and fluting phrases flashing into the still air, like sunlight bouncing off polished chrome.

The last light spills across the fields, seemingly reflected from the dark clouds above and intensified, like optical acoustics, giving depth to rich and resonant colours. Overhead a pair of great black-backed gulls head for their roost, their deep querulous calls sounding as if they are chuntering to each other about some perceived grievance. Reed warblers gossip; a resonant harmonic of the rustling reeds. A short-eared owl hangs low over the saltmarsh grasses on stiff outstretched wings. It turns sharply and skims downwind, then turns back into the breeze, now with slow, deep, fluid wingbeats. Its eyes are set deep within its large head, flat-faced like a radar dish. Its glowing amber irides, punctured by the black discs of wide-open pupils, peer steadily into the base of the vegetation. Yet hunting ahead of the night holds its own dangers, for it is accosted by two herring gulls. Far more agile than its pursuers, it out-climbs and out-turns them, but the chase attracts more gulls and as the odds become overwhelming it pitches down sharply into tall grass. Darkness is not far away; it can wait. On the horizon, where the day's embers have been doused, pinpoints of electric light begin to glimmer. A rabbit startles and dashes along the base of hedge, white tail pumping as it goes. Inky-blue twilight deepens from the east, spotless and smooth before the stars appear, yet translucent and glowing, Venus the only beacon. Suddenly the swallows have gone. Far across the fields, a blackbird sings its final madrigal and falls silent. The hush of the gloaming insinuates itself into the consciousness which pauses and listens to the stillness. A cow coughs harshly, a touchstone to reality amongst the surreal shadows of the gathering gloom.

Night falls softly but with unease. As the hours pass, thunder grumbles in the distance; a pheasant crows in response. A blackbird chooks softly in anxiety in the darkness. Reed warblers fret and prattle in the thick warm sticky night; their songs, streams of introspection, disjointed and rambling, fading and fading and fading and then suddenly jerking back loudly as if they have remembered something else they wanted to say to themselves. Away over the river, dim sheet lightning licks and flickers flat between the clouds like a fusillade of distant artillery, the muzzle flashes curiously silent until thunder rolls in haltingly from the horizon, deep and prolonged, growing and growing then dying slowly away – yin to the reed warblers' yang. As the storm nears, the sky flashes silver and grey, peach and black, each barrage of thunder answered by growls from another cloud like an angry animal pawing at the ground; the ancients flinging brimstone across the heavens. Overhead, the sky is rent by multiple forked lightning grounding all around, stabbing earthward with numbing concussions. Its ferocity changes night into day for the briefest of moments, but it is unnatural light, vivid violent and jarring, light that casts no shadows but plunges the eyes into blackness until their retinal refractory period ceases and vision is restored. The sour tang of arcing voltage sits sharp on the tongue from the electrocuted air. There is no rain. For half an hour the storm drifts across the sky, slipping slowly eastwards inland until once again the lightning flashes in silence. Quite suddenly the humid warmth is replaced by crisp chill from the passing front. Stars reappear. In the settled air, the falsetto yap of a dog fox bounces from the distant blackness to be answered closer by a vixen's shriek that curdles the night. Nearby, a barn owl calls, a primeval wavering scream, ragged at the edges, shocking in its suddenness, frightening in its unearthliness. Slowly, the silence courses back, recomposing itself, yet somehow now with an edge of watchfulness in the darkness; a silence hearkening for a noise, like a child left at home for the first time listening for monsters on the stairs.

The sky is suddenly full of swallows. They have been feeding low over a newly topped pasture all morning, with many recently fledged juveniles clutching the tops of the flailed thistle stems as they rest between their first serious bouts of flight. Three yellow wagtails, feeding on the same glut of insects, have frequently had to duck those skimming at grass level. Yet suddenly the swallows have coalesced into one area of the sky as if drawn by a centripetal force. They fly erratically, some making exaggerated undulations, climbing high into the sky as if trying to escape from the unseen vortex yet flipping over into steep dives drawn inexorably back to its centre. Twittering crescendos around them. The reason for their convergence dashes from behind a line of willows, a curving rush of muted blue slicing through the air on sharp bowed wings. The hobby glides fast with barely a wingbeat, lissom, skimming the sky with that graceful ease that comes from suppressed power, like a cheetah padding softly ahead of a sprint. It rises above the harsh alarm calls of the parent swallows, hearing them only after it has passed, the calls pursuing it and fading as it searches for easy prey. With effortless speed, it closes its wings yet climbs steeply in a way that even the swallows need to beat their wings hard to achieve, rotating, its slate-blue upperparts becoming striped pale underparts becoming slate-blue again as it revolves on its vertical upward trajectory. It rolls out and arcs gracefully through the top of a parabola, plunging back through the swallow flock, bright yellow talons outspread seeking to sift warm flesh from the streaming air. It finds none. Levelling out low over the pasture, it turns sharply and begins to rise again, but this time the hunter is hunted, for the swallows have converged tightly around it, closing down its air space, claustrophobic in their presence, shrill in their spiked noise, shutting down all room for manoeuvre. It sheds motion and lands abruptly in the mid-branches of the tortured twistedness of a dead hawthorn, colour appearing, catching up with it, infusing its shape, flaring in the brightness. Sunlight dances inside its eyes, deep and dark and glistening. It blinks, its nictitating membrane blanking its eye momentarily, and turns its head away, refocusing. It raises a foot to its beak and inspects it closely as if to confirm that it has indeed not caught food. Yet. For seemingly, again without a wingbeat, the hobby is suddenly airborne once more and gliding swiftly, trimming up into another vertical climb, the swallows that had in their overconfidence left it alone in the hedge now flailing in its wake as they try to enforce the same blanket suppression. But this time the falcon slips away, disappearing behind another hedge out by the riverbank, and the swallows diffuse back over the pastures to feed.

Dawn is a morning away; the igneous fissure that scorched crimson the eastern horizon of the massed grey clouds is long past, but the clouds remain. Only now, the ephemeral architecture of the sky has changed through the morning from rumpled featureless softness pierced by an occasional slanting sunbeam to towering turrets of glinting alabaster actively sculpted by the high air seething upward on the approaching cold front. Below, they are spongy and wet, soft like brushfuls of watercolour pigment dabbed on wet paper, pale pearl where the hidden sun penetrates clefts, dark graphite on the flat bases of the denser tumuli. There is no wind. The air is warm and dank. Moisture cleaves to skin. Sunlight gleams dully: tarnished silver light that throws no shadows, brightening or darkening almost imperceptibly as the upper clouds shift above. Rain is intermittent, the soft rain of summer, plump drops that seem to fall slowly with lots of space between; more like warm tears than rain, wetting only slightly, a brief film of dampness that dries quickly, recycled into the cloying humidity.

The light is green, wafted up and trapped by the heavy charcoal vapour draped above. The river coruscates like a rapier thrust deep into the verdant heart of the fields. Cattle are somnolent, ruminating with bovine impassiveness, most slumped in the grass with a few standing all tightly together in one corner of the pasture. The yellow carpets of buttercups are gone from the hay meadows, replaced by yellow cushions of bird's-foot trefoil and the rising pink haze of the sheep's sorrel. Butterflies flitter and float; bumblebees are busy at the nodding cerise pompoms of the musk thistles. Swallows have deserted the stillness of the cattle to sweep over the swards, slowing to just above a stall with tail streamers spread to snatch flies startled from the landing pads of white umbels hoisted above the grass panicles by the cow parsley. Palpitations of apprehension swell in the corner of a field. A whitethroat churrs harshly and insistently from a bramble bush; a male blackbird shakes with consternation on a fencepost, its fanned tail lifted high above its back, its wings flicking, its legs bouncing, scolding agitatedly. Rabbits stand alert, erect on hind legs, casting a watchful gaze at the chestnut ripple of a weasel flowing along a grass track through the field.

Disquiet is also present on the saltmarsh, for gulls are rising. It takes a lot to spook a great black-backed gull but the dark hulking form of a female marsh harrier will do it. She hangs low over the riverbank, gazing deeply into the vegetation. A hefty ponderous bird with hunched muscular shoulders, she has a deceptively leisurely flight, yet is capable of astonishing agility. She floats on long broad wings held just above her back, wallowing on the beginnings of a breeze, occasionally beating her wings heavily to avoid stalling, rocking in the instability that slow flight brings, then gliding long in calmer air. Her plumage is burnished the colour of muscovado sugar with a golden crown. She swings shallowly away from the bank, then makes a change of direction so sudden that it is as if a few frames in a film have been missed as the result of a bad edit, a ninety-degree turn executed so swiftly and with such deftness as to belie the weight of her body. She resumes her deliberate progress along the bank then pauses in a clumsy hover, tail spread and wings working desperately to keep her aloft, long yellow legs dangling loosely below her. Suddenly she collapses into the vegetation and the ear listens for the gunshot that never comes. Half a minute becomes a minute and she rises from the stillness once more, phoenix-like, reincarnated from the crumpled mass of feathers that fell, but her talons hold no prey and she resumes her languid progress along the bank. Knowing that the harrier is a ground hunter and that flight is the best defence, the mixed flock of gulls rise lazily from their roost ahead of her path, unfazed but cautious, and drift out to the mud leaving just a few pied wagtails on the short sheep-cropped turf, trotting and bobbing and dipping and wagging as they snatch insects from the grass, unperturbed by the harrier's passage.

From the mouth of a green tunnel under the dark stolidity of hawthorns and the paler motion of the willows, a pair of foxes appear into the liquid light of the meadow. They slope out into the grass, heads slunk low, noses sniffing keenly but they are not hunting; they have come to play. Skittish and frisky, they face each other, leaping up to interlock black paws and white jaws, bucking and twisting, rolling over together in the long grass, eight feet raised to the sky with puppy-like abandon. They lie that way, together, like a pair of young lovers might, amongst the summer flowers staring at the sky and their dreams to come. Then it is back to play with a blithe innocence, jumping up at each other, front legs waving and grappling, play-biting at each other's muzzles. They stop occasionally to stare around, parabolic ears cocked, just to reassure themselves that they are indeed alone, their white-tipped tails, thick and lustrous, twitching in unison. Then chasing. First bounding joyously one after the other, then side by side; then stopping to sit quietly with each other almost invisible in the longer grass at the base of the hedgerow, before more wrestling, pushing and pawing at each other's white bibs, falling and frolicking like young parents that have found time to re-kindle the innocent intimacy of first love. They leave the field quietly, the vixen first, the dog loitering briefly to scent mark the flattened grass of their private playground, before following her back through the green tunnel to the onerous reality of rearing their cubs.

Midsummer's morn rises cool and pallid and still, layered between days of baking heat from sunny blue skies and a southerly air mass born distantly in Iberia. The dawn chorus is hushed, the breathy exhalations of woodpigeons heavy and cloying and soporific like an aural opiate. They are augmented only by the occasional syncopated backing harmonics of collared doves and the stock doves' hollow rhythmic pumping, soft yet insistent like the morning's heartbeat. A distant cockerel's call jolts with discordance. Light is harsh and white and glassy. The sea is flat, its eternal restlessness muted, softened to little palpitations along its edge; motion denied. In pastures bleached and crisped under recent days of sun cattle graze ahead of the coming incalescence, swallows wheeling tight patterns around them as they trawl for disturbed insects. Sunshine swirls and leaps across the tall grass in the meadows and falls into the shadow crevasses that the early morning breeze breaks open through their surface. It looks as if the sound of the breeze in the grass should be audible yet the eddies are silent. Then from deep within the sward a sound of yesteryear emanates, the urgent insistent three-note plea of a calling quail.

Morning ages, cloud dissipates, sunlight intensifies; the heat becomes tropical, corralled into pockets with firebreaks of cooler breeze between. The cattle are sitting, now waiting out the trial-by-heat of another day. Ears twitch and tails flick to keep the relentless clouds of buzzing flies at bay. Farmers start work, the roar and whine of a tractor-mounted grass-cutter shattering the stillness as it moves in parallel strips through the distortions of the rising heat haze, savagely reducing swaying grass to inert hay, harsh straight stripes appearing in a land of soft shapes, intrusive in their regimentation. A hare bounds between the rows just spawned as its familiar vertical and closed world becomes bewilderingly flat and open. The cutting takes just minutes and the tractor moves away to fields anew, literally making hay while the sun shines. Afterwards, the air above is full of swallows as if the soul of the grasses' movement has transmuted into flight; the inert cut grass now dead and drying, full of crows and magpies, all feasting on the disturbed insects. In the lane, a cacophony of bleating rises as sheep are herded from field to shed for their annual shearing. Heat haze broils over the griddle that the mudflats have become. Two swifts scythe low over the pastures; longer-winged than the swallows with faster wingbeats, they possess a tautness not found in other birds; an inner energy, tense like a coiled watch spring that never unwinds. Their flight shimmers. From a nearby hedge, a Cetti's warbler explodes its stentorian song into the air like sonic shrapnel. Across the river, the muffled hum of traffic on the distant motorway intrudes, borne on the hot southerly breeze to touch the edge of consciousness, hinting at the frenetic activity of a world much more remote from this tranquillity than just the few miles between them.

Recently moved to pastures fresh, cattle lie lethargically amongst tall grass chewing cud beneath afternoon skies gravid with dark grey rain. The hedges are lush and viridescent, leaves heavy in the still air, damp from earlier drizzle. The southerly air mass is thick and moist, tropically oppressive leaving all short of breath save the woodpigeons whose endless drowsy crooning reverberates softly across the fields. Distantly, the high tide pants rhythmically. A grass snake uncoils itself from the short grass at the edge of an eroded mole caldera where it has been trying to bask. Its scales are opaquely lustred, tawny-olive on its upper side with a pale lemon and black collar, the same colours barred along its flanks. Its head is flat with a narrow cream ring around the inner edge of its black iris highlighting the perfect circle of its depthless black pupil. It slides away in curiously motionless undulations, exact replications of its pattern of sinuous waves reappearing repeatedly every few seconds, creating an illusion of stillness to its forward motion as if its whole body is carried by unseen cilia. Its black forked tongue flickers ahead of it, tasting the silent language around that only it can interpret. It swaps green land for emerald water as it swims through the duckweed on the surface of a pond, its whole body submerged with only its head held clear like a snorkel. It disappears, leaving a momentary impression of its being in a narrow wake of silver ripples.

Above, an emperor dragonfly patrols low over the same pond, its four lattice-veined transparent wings crackling like rain falling on high-voltage power cables. Their synchronised flickering is powered by a heavy apple-green thorax, the long powder-blue abdomen trailing like a fuselage, the twin green globular eyes like turrets, menacing like an opaline insect-gunship. Initially its flight appears to be random, but it is quartering the pond systematically, flying at constant height and speed in long straight lines with sharp about-turns, each one accompanied by the rattle of its wings, that put it on a reverse parallel track, back and forth, forth and back, like a sentry on guard duty; but instead of guarding it is hunting. Yet like the sentry, it is interception that it is seeking. The cloying dank depths of the surrounding reedbed emits a high-pitched croak and disgorges a moorhen from its vertical miasma. White flashes under its tail flick in time with its steps. A satellite of black fluff orbits it irregularly, occasionally intersecting to touch beaks for food. Together they launch into the thick vibrant carpet of duckweed, opening bottomless black crevasses in the pond's surface, as the chick learns to pick at titbits while the adult supplements it with choice morsels. Above, in another plane that the moorhens will never know, a reed warbler crepitates in its newly verdant world, the line of new green reeds that has risen throughout spring having now reached the top and replaced last year's bleached bent stems. Its song, narrow-pitched with a snare drum quality, is far-reaching and insistent, ever about to end yet ever jerking away with a new phrase and cadence, an ancient cantillation preached only to summer skies.

Pink paints the upper sky, stretched thin, faint like dye on wet chiffon. A week after the solstice, and morning is aqueous, the clouds crowded and muscular, reminders of recent rain and prophets of more. There is no dawn chorus today, just a single blackbird singing in the chill wetness. Its song shines dully, fading fast like a fresh-cut face of sodium, dispersing quickly in the sodden air like a single drip of milk into water. The notes come endlessly but with no overlap, each discrete, waiting patiently in line, rising like a single stream of bubbles in a glass of flat beer. Deflated woodpigeons pump a few phrases into the air as if trying to inflate punctured bagpipes, then succumb to the futility and fall silent. Song is now less of a priority than finding sufficient food for young: the territorial imperative stymied. Yet for some, their young are already independent. Flurries of immature starlings blow across the fields in squalls animating the otherwise quiet landscape. Gangs of these gawky and garrulous juveniles have been growing over the preceding weeks to number hundreds or even thousands. They are starting to garner the first signs of adulthood as newly-moulted oily green wing coverts and white-tipped dark body feathers begin to replace the greyish-fawn uniformity of juvenile plumage. Uncontrolled by the few adults present, amid a cacophony of raucous chattering they wheel and dive chaotically between the fields and the trees and the house roof, investigating everything with the fearless inquisitiveness of youth. Frequently one will fall down the chimneys into the cold fireplaces of summer having navigated the recesses of the H-pots and subverted the wire baffles placed to prevent their entry. Descending *en masse* to areas of short turf, they displace the birds already present, their constant noise and squabbling too much for the sedately feeding blackbirds and the house sparrows dust-bathing on the dry molehills; they flee into adjacent hedges. Then away. As suddenly as they appeared the starlings take once more to the wing only to dive into the next field amongst the tall grass and thistle stems to disappear like snowflakes melting on water; but then another eruption as they move to the bramble hedge and then on into another field and another, a constant pulse that will be repeated every few hours as they complete some random circuit.

In the drizzle of late morning, a dog fox stalks cautiously through a tall hay meadow. His wet fur is dark and matted. He stops, cocking his black ears, then leaps and pounces in a liquid rufous arc. But no luck, no vole, no meal. Undeterred he tries again and then again but still no capture. He walks away and sits amongst the pink haze of the sorrel as if in contemplation, gazing intently as he turns his head back and forth. He stands and shakes his fur, releasing a silver corona that shimmers momentarily around him. He trots towards the garden, seemingly nonchalant yet accelerates rapidly around the end of the wall scattering young rabbits ahead of him. White scuts flash distress, practice games now tested in deadly earnest. For one, too few games, too little practice, there will be no more   but the fox has his meal. He crunches sharply, transforming a cute head into a formless pink mass. He eats leisurely, turning the carcass occasionally, using a paw to help dismember it. When he has half-eaten it, he stands and carries the remains in his mouth to a corner of the garden. He digs a hole in the sandy soil and lays the body carefully there and covers it – what resembles a ritual burial but is simply a meal for another day. He returns to the site of his meal, licks the blood from the wet grass stems and, with the truculent chatter of magpies berating his every step, walks slowly around the pond and away, swallowed by the incessant drizzle.

Colour drains from the sky as the light dims. Blackbirds chink the foreshadow of nightfall that in high summer comes slowly, the gloaming clinging to the sky, refusing to melt into night. The river glows deep blue as if it has been soaking up the colour from the sky all day and is now releasing it. Low tide, the sea hushed; the heady fragrance of drying hay rising on the soft warm air, thick and heavy, stirred by the lightest of breezes, and silence so deep that you can almost touch it. Flies shimmy in swarms in the lee of bushes like a Brownian ballet. A solitary bat, uncommon here, flutters silently in the indigo air on the desiccated parchment of its wings. In the warmth that never quite seems to dissolve into the chill of night, sedge warblers still etch the air with their jagged chatter. A pregnant moon, swollen and yellow, performs mitosis with its river reflection and cleaves into the translucence of the darkening sky as yet too pale for stars, the twin glimmers of Mercury and Jupiter still the only celestial beacons. Breaking the silence, the kleeping of an oystercatcher, softened and sculpted by distance, ululates from the river's mouth. The wavering song of a curlew skirls through the warm summer night in a forlorn search for answers across the darkened fields. With the light well-nigh gone and the colours muted to a luminous glow, out of the stillness on noiseless wings a little owl beats rapidly across the field to land abruptly on a fence post. It bobs up and down on its feathered legs and stares around, head swivelling like a ventriloquist's dummy as if surprised by where it has materialised. A brooding tension touches the twilight. Its incendiary yellow eyes, lit by an internal fire, flare in the monochrome stillness, searching, searching … and then it is gone as hushed and sudden as was its arrival. And the night relaxes.

JULY
COGITATIONS OF THE DIVINE

Sunlight blows across the fields in constant motion. Hedges are overgrown with summer. Great willowherb is copious along the banks of the rhynes. Its deep cerise flowers bear white cruciform stigma like recent converts displaying their newfound piety for all to see. The fields are a patchwork of greens. In the tall grass of the uncut hay, hazy with yellow and white flowers, small green grasshoppers jump in droves with every footstep. Recently-cut hayfields are lime-green, the aftermath vivid and unnatural, jarring in its brightness. In the softer darker pastures, all but one of the cows lies chewing cud, the exception staring out across the barbed wire fence with baleful brown eyes, lost in a dream beyond enclosure. The End Field is neglected this year, with large stands of pale grey-green musk thistles topped by soft carmine cushions genuflecting in the sun; the ranker creeping thistle abundant. Change is stalking this land, though it does not know it. Age is taking its toll on the farmer and his family; illness and infirmity, concern and care. He holds many fewer sheep this year so several fields have been left ungrazed; the air here no longer bears their bleating, and a faded red tractor, with rusty controls, stands semi-used in the long grass. 'Massey Ferguson 165' says its label, but at least forty summers have passed since it shone from the factory. Thoughts turn to how this pastoral system will change after a lifetime of love and understanding. How will that intimate knowledge, be passed on, if at all? And if not, how will these fields change? Will the fingers of neglect draw tight, or will newer monster machinery bludgeon its sense of order onto a land caressed for three score years and ten?

Yet such change can be discerned only by the long-lived; for everything else it is unnoticed and the focus is on rearing the next generation. The Farm is a microcosm of this fecundity. House sparrows and blue tits carry food from flowers in the front garden to young fledged from holes in the cobbled walls, left with care when they were repointed. A male pied wagtail feeds a washed-out short-tailed miniature of itself perched on the porch. Behind the planted windbreak, small family parties of greenfinches and goldfinches have come together, twittering ceaselessly, to feed on the seeds of weeds growing at the edges of the rows of vegetables. Robins feed brown-spotted juveniles perched amongst seldom-used machinery in the open barns, while above them woodpigeons, stock doves and collared doves occupy nests on concrete beams or crevices where walls meet roofs. A swallow plunges into the cool shade of the barn, sweeping up to its half-nest on the cobweb-covered rafters, there met by a flare of yellow gapes in the shrouded dimness. Sweet chitterings fill the silence as the swallow empties its bulging brick-red crop into the insatiable depths of its young, then it drops away to sweep through the ancient gap of the threshing door in a sparkle of blue.

There is more at play, however, than simply filling every brightly-coloured gape with as much food as is possible; more subtle strategies invoked to maximise genes passed into the next generation. A male blackbird busies itself collecting worms from the lawn, packaging them tidily as they heave and wriggle and strain against the brutal bonds of its saffron mandibles. It heads towards a flower bed, there to be met by a well-grown fledgling, sombre brown with pale feather shafts above and darker spotting below. It has been making haphazard attempts to feed itself beneath the cover of a rose bush, but as its father approaches it races towards him, mouth agape, screaming shrilly, wings fluttering frantically, demanding to be fed. Yet the male hops around it, ignoring its pleas, and finds a sibling sitting quietly in a nearby clump of flowers and deposits his cargo deep into its yellow yawn. He returns to the lawn to forage further, the original fledgling following, venturing away from the cover behind it, picking at various items and occasionally swallowing one. The male, now with another beakful of food, heads towards a different flowerbed, again carefully navigating past its insistent youngster, to feed a third member of its brood. Back and forth, back and forth, the male goes in a ceaseless toil to feed its two offspring that are quite big enough to feed themselves, yet always ignoring the imploring juvenile that follows it around. Finally, the male's mate appears with food and flies directly to this ostracised fledgling, pushing mixed invertebrates deep into its gape that threatens to swallow the mother in its eagerness for food.

She flies a short distance away and the youngster follows, now being fed most of the food items that she finds, for this is one of her babies – blackbird parents divide their final brood of the season between them at the point of fledging and refuse to feed each other's babies however insistent they may be. As with many birds, they also control the point that their youngsters gain independence by altering the frequency of their feeding; when a juvenile can achieve a higher rate of energy intake by feeding itself than by begging from a parent, it stops begging. Early in spring, when the male looks after all the fledglings and the female readies herself to lay another brood, he will reduce his rate of feeding early so that the young become independent about two weeks after fledging, but in midsummer, unencumbered by their decision not to raise a further brood, they can extend this period to over three weeks, thereby providing greater investment into the long-term survival of what could be their last ever offspring.

Afternoon, green and peaceful; warmth and quietness stretch across the fields to the river. The air is thick and syrupy, distant sounds brought close in the humidity building in the shadows of darkening cloud. Above, silvered turrets sweep heavenward like coral reefs developed over millennia, here produced simply in moments. From far in the distance a gentle rumble provides a premonition. In the proximity of the fields there is subtle unease. Woodpigeons pause briefly from their feeding to look around, cows raise their heads and sniff the air, a blackbird chooks softly from a hedge, a male pheasant stretches hard and crows harsh and loudly then shakes itself vigorously, fluffing its feathers as it returns to feed; merest intimations of possibilities to come. And come it gradually does, almost imperceptible yet inexorable. The soft breeze stills, no breath of wind now stirs the thickening silence, broken only as distant thunder drums the rim of the horizon, reverberating from the ground below, a wounded resentful sound.

The storm drifts slowly from the south, approaching across the river, heavy and malevolent, the sky now violet-black, the fields fluorescent in the sunlight flooding from under them bringing clarity to the horizon; distance briefly sharply focused. It advances tentatively, shards of crackling electricity flickering brightly in the darkness from cloud to ground, its reptilian tongue tasting the way ahead. Swifts are the storm-bringers; those trawlers of the aerial plankton have been evicted from the brilliant vaults of the high air above the hills and towns and now flee the downdraughts in the dank and darkening basement air of the hollows over the fields. They are silent here, their extravagant screaming stifled, yet still they revel on the eddying air currents, riding the bow waves of the storm. Nervousness has become a contagion: young Friesian cattle skip in the fields while older ones stand, heads turned towards the rolling thunder. Collared doves flutter and croon, repeatedly alighting apprehensively on a wall before taking flight again – small balls of agitation, heartbeats awry with primeval angst in the face of unbridled power and undirected energy. Lark song is extinguished. Wind gusts, tugging at the hedgerows, the storm's frigid breath touching all. Flocks of hirundines skim low over the fields, escaping the oncoming onslaught. A little egret coruscates overhead, white against the blackness of the cloud. The storm clouds press down, concentrating all life to an increasingly damp, narrow band of air as if trying to reverse evolution and force beasts of land and air back into the water. Eventide comes prematurely as the light dies over the fields. Sheet lightning flickers and rumbles below the unseen thunderhead, while fizzling bolts cleave the pink-tinged lower sky, leaving rent eyesight flashing red and green negative facsimiles, rent air booming across the distance.

Suddenly, the first flecks of rain spatter from the heavens, bloated and lethargic, lifting coronas of dust from the impact craters in the dry pale soil, darkening it as the moisture is absorbed. The foreshortened horizon hisses, expectation careering ahead of the storm which arrives violently – a sucking vortex lashing the trees, throwing the reeds into tumult. Hedges buck and writhe like wild animals in agony. Cold rain streams, rushing in the air, thrumming on the ground, shaking leaves, flattening grass, rebounding from the track with fizz. Cattle canter heavily for cover, or in the absence of shelter turn their backs to the stinging rain. Hailstones sugar-coat the fields. A lone lesser black-backed gull glides low on arched wings from the sea to the river, the only being unperturbed by the cacophony around it. It seems to chaperone a flock of curlews across the fields, refugees from the exposed mudflats where the rain hurls sharpened lances at the surface. Their calls are almost lost in the deafening thunder. The normally placid sky has become a place of strange hostility, a constant reverberating kaleidoscope of crashing booms and tremors. Rain slants in dark veils across the glistening mud, obliterating horizons that just a moment ago were clear and sharp, as the ragged edge of the storm rolls northwards across the saltings, the darting tongues of voltage still licking at their surface.

From above, the continuous salvoes of thunder now resonate with a deeper pitch, the sound-shift announcing that the storm has passed overhead. Malice slowly recedes. Angst lifts. Swifts rise and vanish. As the rumbling recedes, cows recommence their grazing. The bottom edge of the maelstrom becomes fringed white like an ermine border to a dark robe. The rain finally ceases, and evening lightens with a second dawn. Trees still. Reeds calm. The sky quietens. The mudflats glisten after the deluge as the eastern hills emerge from the purple-washed clouds. Gulls, waders and cormorants return from the river's shelter to the coastal mudflats as the thunder rolls away to distant shores. Cattle disperse once more across the meadows. The sticky cloying humidity has gone, replaced with freshness and the rising smell of sweet grass. An autumnal mist steams into the cold air, swaddling the fields in white wisps, a physical manifestation of evaporating concern.

The soft light of morning has aged into the harsher light of afternoon. Cumulus are growing in the rising heat radiating from the ground, scaling the colder heights of the blue air above. The large ones absorb the satellite puffs around them; the big ones bump and merge, filaments of each reaching out to touch and intertwine, embracing like old friends, coalescing, the night's thunderheads forming. Swallows feed high. Swifts feed higher, parties already congregating beneath the birth pangs of the storms. Gulls circle, black against the dazzling white summits. The rising warmth of the land pulls in cooler air from offshore, and the sea breeze streams through the meadow, rippling the tall grass in silvered waves, touching it gently with an invisible hand like fingers stroking the fur of a pet cat, depressing it with their touch, making it pale and silky before it rebounds, dark and lustrous, with the passing pressure, that darkening itself echoing the fleeting shadows of the drifting clouds above. The meadow is green now in hue only, for it is heavily suffused tawny from the waving panicles and sheened with burnished copper and soft pink by the flowering sheep's sorrel. The fluffy heads of the meadow soft-grass add pale silvery grey, the cushions of bird's-foot trefoil and the emerging nebulae of autumn hawkbit add yellow; and cerise is studded throughout with red clover, restharrow, and pyramidal orchids. A pill millipede trundles across the edge of a molehill like a minute vulcanised sumo wrestler. Meadow browns flit through the forest of grass stems, the females flashing orange on their forewings.

A caterpillar of a large white butterfly, yellow-green with black longitudinal stripes made up from rectangles on each segment, climbs a grass stem, exploring a route with its three front legs, and hauling its soft body heavily up behind it. It searches side branches where leaves diverge, but continues up the main stalk, using its stumpy anal prolegs like a neotropical monkey uses its prehensile tail. The stem is already heavy with flowers, the anthers rich in pink pollen ready to be disgorged to the wind. As the caterpillar reaches this high canopy its added weight causes the delicate stem to flex and bend, so that as it continues to ascend it is actually heading earthward. Buffeted by the breeze, it nearly loses all footing, and wraps its body around the shaft to prevent a fall, then continues gingerly to the very end. There, it reaches out and crosses to another stalk and begins to climb again, the released stem immediately springing upright. The new grass is taller, emerging above the main sward, and as the caterpillar ascends it casts around from side to side appearing to look down as if concerned as to how high it has climbed; yet something drives it on. Its movement is slower now, navigating the spiky panicles more difficult than the single smooth stem that holds them aloft. It searches each crevice between the flowers assiduously, but appears not to find what it is looking for. Finally, it reaches the summit, and holding tight with all its prolegs it waves its head around futilely, for this is as high into the air as it will reach until it develops wings. Whatever it might have been searching for it has failed to find. It turns around. The descent will be a long one.

At the edge of another meadow below the riverbank, where poppies dab scarlet in the taller margins, a female rabbit suckles her five kits at the entrance of her sandy burrow. They are star rabbits, a local genetic trait that bequeaths a white beauty spot on their foreheads. They scramble ferociously to get underneath her, bucking her into the air as she struggles to stay upright. One is bowled onto its back, but refuses to let go of her nipple, rear paws kicking frantically in the air as if pedalling a bicycle. Over the bank, the saltmarsh is flat in a world of laminates: the grass is cropped as short as baize by sheep in summer and wildfowl in winter, and hence is never ruffled by the breeze. Bleached bone-white boulders of sleeping shelduck dot its surface, with more gregarious gatherings grouped around the salt-encrusted margins of long-forgotten pools. At its edge, where it falls away in great curving cliffs to the dark wetness of the river as if gouged by a giant spoon, the fine fescues give way to coarser grasses and the pale purple stars of greater sea-spurrey. Below them the upper mud has dried to a concrete-grey and formed large irregular platelets curling at their edges like giant scales. They are separated by deep dark cracks akin to the fissures in eroding glaciers or limestone pavements. They lie above brown valleys lacerated by side gullies, all denuded of vegetation by the regular inundations of the tides. This is a soft sinuous landscape formed by the settling of suspended solids from the slow waters of the rising river, and eroded and moulded by the faster-flowing drainage of low tide. The faded lifeless exoskeleton of a mud-crab lies head-down at the edge of the grass as if trying to burrow into the sediment one last time. It is lightweight, empty of flesh and empty of life, just a husk of chitin still holding the shape of a crab but with barely more substance than a ghost.

Deep dusk, and low down the day is faltering. Circling the distant horizon, ashen clouds smoke in decaying plumes, muting the colours of the setting sun. Yet in the china-blue transparency of the high air, the light still lifts with brightness. Echelons of gulls wing serenely through the softening summer sky on their way to roost in the bay, their flight frictionless and flowing. Seen from the ground they are bright, the adults' whiteness almost translucent, tinged and glowing with the refracted delicate film of the sunset, but as they look down from the last of the day's rays, the land is silhouetted, pitch-black, cloven by the coiled meanders at the end of the glittering river leading like a gilded pathway to the Eldorado of the gleaming mudflats beyond and the glistening dagger of the channel thrust into the side of sleeping England.

In the grass I lie
And watch the gulls soar and fly
On wings translucent to the sky
Drifting aimlessly on high

And as pigeons croon their lullabies
And swallows dip chasing the flies
I try to remember summers past
Yet fogginess leaves me downcast

So sad the ravages of time
That strip cognition from its prime
When cantilevered thoughts would shine
And recall had not yet declined

No more the memories remain
Rising like bubbles from champagne
No longer is the past vibrant
But lost behind befuddlement

The thoughts that travel to the stars
Are still within my repertoire
It's just no longer can I share
Them locked in shadows of despair

And as enfeeblement spreads cold
its hyphae through a brain grown old
In the grass I lie
And watch the gulls … and cry.

The afternoon stretches away into summer, as summer itself is ageing. Heat hangs heavy. Haze blurs the landscape like the disappointment of camera shake. The limpid blue sky is criss-crossed by vapour trails of six-mile-high jets heading for far continents and encroached in the west by curving cirrus, combed like hair by the upper currents. The seeds have gone from the tall bleached grass of the late hay meadow, either fallen or eaten by the finches and sparrows. Lady's bedstraw still flowers in yellow turrets in places, along with the amethyst heads of musk thistle, white corymbs of yarrow, and yellow puffs of autumn hawkbit, all busy with the intricate iridescence of common blues and shimmering small coppers, flaring six-spot burnets, and the sombre tones of the larger but now tatty meadow browns. Four magpies chatter in a pasture amongst the reclining rheumy-eyed cattle that flick their ears and tails constantly in a futile attempt to rid themselves of the persistent biting flies. A blackbird, fleeing the bushes and scolding in alarm, startles a woodpigeon that flushes with an applause of clapping wings. Soft orange flickers up from camouflaged brown as a painted lady rises from the pebbles on the coast path where it has been basking in the sunlight – a visitor from countries south feeling at home in the heat. The southerly breeze rustles the luxuriant reedbed where reed and sedge warblers still stutter desultorily from deep within the foliage, but their voices are subdued as if tired from their summer-long ramblings. Beyond and above, a single brilliant white yacht drifts silently, heeled away from the wind, far out on the mud-coloured sea.

On the foreshore the sea couch-grass is flowering, the heavy green heads revealing cream, filamentous, fork-tipped anthers, a delicate tracery casting billions of pollen grains to the breeze to play the lottery of life. A skylark climbs singing listlessly, and then gives up, dropping directly back into the grass. The days of advertising a territory are nearly at an end;

a more sociable period will soon begin. The saltmarsh lies still and hot. Pools are shrinking in the heat, causing little egrets here to replace their active hunting with a stand-and-wait strategy more akin to that of a nearby grey heron, hunched meditatively amongst its plumes, reflecting on its reflection. A compelling trilling calls attention to a common sandpiper as it flickers low across another pool. Its flight seems clipped, for it never raises its wings above the horizontal as it flitters fast between drooping glides. Only a visitor here, its presence announces that less than a month after the longest day the first of the southbound migrants are already returning. On the opalescent mudbanks of the falling river, hundreds of black-headed gulls seem to trade insults, their carping calls managing to harangue even nothingness on a beautiful afternoon. Shelduck loaf in the sunshine. Some preen, dislodging moulted body feathers that roll across the sand in the breeze like tumbleweed. But most just sleep. Motionless, with bottle-green heads and scarlet bills withdrawn beneath pied wings, their white bodies gleam like porcelain, curved shapes sculpted smooth as if life at the edge of the sea has eroded all angles to leave them rounded like boulders on a shingle beach.

The world seems to slumber, not with the boredom of winter but with a carefree restfulness, a time to lie back and recuperate from the stress of raising families. Only the ever-skimming swallows and the wafting reeds show signs of movement, with the soft lavender heat haze shimmering over them like immiscible liquid, melting their seed heads into the distant mud. But the reality is like the haze, just a mirage. A stoat ripples from the edge of tall grass pursuing a fleeing white tail; a little egret stalks across the mudflats in pursuit of crabs; a kestrel hovers patiently to dive-bomb a vole; even the swallows' innocuous slaloms are actually dogfights after insects. All this and more – the blue tit hanging upside down gleaning insects from a hawthorn; the dragonflies quartering rhynes on rattling wings; life and death continuing to be played out all around. Yet in summer, warmed by sunshine and caressed by soft wind, these battles are disguised under a blanket of lethargy. But the fall streaks of cirrus are slowly giving way to stratus flooding east from the western hills out across the flatlands, cutting the sun's warmth, and the wind is changing – no longer thermic, but now a strengthening westerly breeze. Rain is coming, unseen and as yet too far to smell, but rain is coming. It is written in the sky.

Rain has hushed the land throughout the night with its constant lullaby. The ground lies wet in the sultry morning air, the soil dark, the vegetation lustrous. Late hay has been delayed again. The decaying remnants of last night's rain clouds lie low and dark across the eastern horizon. Overhead, cloud is breaking; light is luminous, liquid sunlight dazzles, wet grass winks silver. The still air is heavy, the quiescence pervasive, the humidity seeming to absorb sound. A pair of carrion crows and their youngsters sit on the roof of a barn, beaks pulled to their breasts like four cowled monks hunched in a dawn vigil. From far away another crow's caw rolls though the last of the drizzle, and a few twitters from low-flying swallows jab feebly at the thick-skinned silence like blunt needles of sound. A woodpigeon coos throatily from a fence post close by, the sound sudden and startling, rolling away in waves, rough and rasping like a domestic cat's tongue. A hare folds into the bejewelled grass, long ears flat against its back, fur wet and sleeked, hugging the contours of the earth so that just the top arch of its body shows above the vegetation, like a molehill. It remains tense and crouched as a russet undulation ceases movement and the black tip of a tail catches up, the whole morphing into a stoat. It stops and stands erect on its back legs, immaculate white underparts showing like some archetypical fluffy toy, its black beady eyes concentrating its intelligence as it searches over the top of the sward. Then it flows again, looping through the wet grass stems, making precision contact with the earth in a series of arcs like a seamstress tacking stitches, before disappearing below a bramble hedge, atop which an immature reed bunting agitates, flicking its white outer tail feathers like semaphore flags. In a hawthorn, above a rhyne where spires of purple loosestrife rise like minarets, a willow warbler whistles. The first of the year's terrestrial migrants, it slurs its two soft notes together almost as one; the sound is compelling but its source is hard to glimpse amongst the dappled shadows of the dense leaves.

From high over the riverbank come waders' calls, burning from the unconscious registration of sound to the conscious recognition of whimbrels. Piercing the quietude, insistent as a morning alarm yet insubstantial as a dawn mist, their stuttering ripples skitter from the fraying shrouds of grey, telling tales of the tundra. At first the sky is empty, but slowly as the calls grow louder the southbound flock becomes visible, farther away than expected, the ventriloquial and penetrating quality of the voices deceiving the searching eye. Smaller and shorter-billed than their curlew cousins, the loose flock of thirteen birds is effervescent, buoyant and mobile in form, seemingly bound together only by the continual tittering of their taut calls. They are the quintessential sound of movement, of temporary being, for this species is always but a fleeting visitor, the birds rarely staying more than a few days, always at the edge of land and water, the sounds always at the edge of consciousness, always tremulous, seemingly brittle as if each might snap before ending. At the point, over two thousand shelduck loaf on the glittering sand, their numbers rising ahead of their annual moult. At the edge of the waves, fifty-seven curlew and a single dunlin, its belly still ink-stained, stand sleepily, some more arrivals back from northern lands where they have probably failed to breed successfully.

The hot cloudless afternoon slips into gentle evening. The sea breeze stills. Quietness rises like invisible mist over the fields, condensing, dampening the distance, thickening the immediacy of the present. Shadows thrown by the lowering sun finger out across the fields, embracing them tentatively like an inexperienced young lover. At the foot of the riverbank in a short-grazed pasture from which cows have recently been removed, a pair of roe deer graze warily, never moving too far from the security of the bushy bank, frequently raising heads and swivelling ears to search for signs of danger. The sky suffuses with the intense pink of forced rhubarb. The sun sinks towards the hazy sea, winking green as its final circumference dips below the tangent of the horizon, signalling the end of another day. In the gloaming, as tranquillity gathers her skirts around, and with the cooling air softly silky on the skin, the colours of twilight intensify in that moment before dusk wraps its velvet cloak of intimacy around the final minutes of the day. Owl-dawn comes with liquid darkness. In the calm, the world slumbers under a totally clear sky, still with remnants of blue at the edges, darkening at the apex into an inky indigo, the first stars just blinking into existence, flickering with time and distance. The twinkling light, emitted hundreds of years before, has travelled across the immensity of space to be extinguished here on this warm night. The night-time sun kisses the day-old moon with the slimmest of silver crescents, and with the beacon of Venus moored above there is seemingly absolutely nothing but nothing between us and other worlds. In the silence is that sense of awe and wonder spawned in all who have gazed upwards since the birth of humankind, alone in the immensity of the universe; that moment in time and space, that for unfathomable reasons you know that you will return to time and again, and the here and now will reform in the future as the question 'Do you remember when …?'; that time when the big questions unanswered through the halls of human history 'Who?' and 'Why?' fleet-footed dance across the surface of the mind, and an unseen finger draws a narrow line of shivers up the back of the neck with primeval cogitations of the divine. And the white owl swells into the night.

Morning blooms blue. It is already warm, presaging heat through the coming day. Swallows feed high, almost beyond vision in the searing brilliance. A greenfinch wheezes asthmatically from high in a hedgerow willow. In the fields, white scuts bob as rabbits move between grazing sites. Meadow browns bask amongst the bedstraws and trefoils. Yarrow stands tall, its white panicles attracting pollinating insects. Nearer the coast, sea bindweed spirals through sea couch-grass to raise its white-shot pink trumpets to the sun like seaside rock. A whitethroat continues to proclaim its territory, even this late in the season, flitting restlessly from perch to perch along the brambles then flying back along the path to start all over again. A newly-independent dunnock perches briefly amongst the bramble flowers, the base of its bill tinged pink like a small girl smudging her mother's lipstick the first time she tries it. Linnets feed on dandelion clocks, disturbing the seed heads in imitation of the children's game 'What time is it?' on a timeless day.

Gulls hang lucent against the flawless sky sewn seamlessly to a sea gleaming like lacquer, lapping almost soundlessly along the beach; rhythm and blue. Sculptured shelduck barely bob. Their numbers are rising as more and more birds arrive at this place of safety for their annual moult. Those riding the slight swell far out in the bay have white rear ends since they have already dropped their black pinions, and those onshore sit through the boredom of waiting to join them in that period of temporary flightlessness while new feathers grow. Small numbers of this year's young have gathered in crèches; off-white or dirty cream with smudges instead of breast bands and conspicuous white cheeks below black hoods, they are gangly and still at times uncoordinated. They appear bemused at the retrograde steps of adults losing the powers that they themselves have only just gained. Amongst them stands a cormorant, not in its heraldic wing-drying pose but dark and brooding and withdrawn, its big webbed feet clamped to the mud. Curlew numbers have also increased sharply overnight, and a flock of two hundred waits out the high tide on the foreshore. For them this is neither home nor the place of safety that the shelduck feel they are in, so they remain alert and edgy, rising into the air at occasional phantom threats. They will be gone in a day or two to distant lands, this shore a mere staging post from which sleek wings will carry them south. Overhead, the first of the black-headed gulls has moulted its name and become white-headed with its fresh plumage.

Behind the shore two young reed warblers churr in the green sea of reeds. On the marsh the pools are largely dry; islands have grown. Adult oystercatchers yelp alarms around sooty-brown youngsters still with remnants of down on their necks and mantles. Nearby older youngsters jump into the air flapping wings, but flight remains elusive and they sit once more; there is still some growing to do. A little egret, immaculately plumed in a tracery of filaments like a wedding veil and regaled in saffron slippers like some pre-midnight Cinderella, forages erratically on the edge of the weed-thickened water, picking items from the surface with surgical precision. It steps sedately out into the shallows, placing its weight on one leg and stirring the muddy bottom gently with the other, head alert, twisting back and forth, black stiletto stabbing reflexively through the surface tension to snatch the freshwater shrimps it has disturbed. It tosses each of them back sharply, gulping them down in a swift fluid motion. Close by on a small island, a male mallard, cross-dressed in his eclipse plumage of moult, shuffles sheepishly deeper into the grass of his hermitage, trying shyly to avoid his secret being discovered; but an uninvited common sandpiper bobs relentlessly on the shore, seemingly determined to draw attention to it.

After days of grey skies and heavy showers, deep blue again vaults overhead, yet even now the air remains unstable, and puffs of white cumulus are swarming from the western hills. The last hayfields remain uncut, well-worn tractors still waiting nearby; but with more rain forecast tomorrow they will remain idle a little longer. A male blackbird sunbathes in the short grass along the side of the coast path. Wings fanned, bill opened skywards, eyes part-closed and glazed, it seems in some sort of delirium, the intoxication of the warmth, like all drugs, bringing oblivion to danger. A reed warbler chatters a short reprise of springtime song in the tops of the gently swaying reeds. The tide slithers in through minute channels in the saltmarsh, worming its way inexorably through the grass, following the irresistible pull of the moon. A small flock of yellow wagtails feed frantically ahead of it, sallying into the air, twisting tightly to catch flies or running quickly across the short turf in that familiar gait, so like clockwork toys. They are mostly immatures with dilute-coloured feathers that will have been replaced prior to their return here, when they will have bloomed into the daffodil yellow of adults. On a gnarled and bleached tree trunk from an unknown forest far away and carried by the current to be deposited at the point by a forgotten winter storm, three wheatears preen. One is still clearly moulting its juvenile plumage; tufts of fluffy down remain around its head like a clown's wig. Like many migrants they are wary and jittery, but the juvenile is the most skittish, frequently jolting away from the log but returning immediately as if on a piece of strong elastic. In the bay, shelduck numbers are peaking; several thousand bob on the high tide that has brought them close to shore like a fringing coral reef. On the southernmost spit of the island a flock of oystercatchers tremble, growing and shrivelling, molten in the roiling heat haze. Most sit dozing with their orange marshalling-baton bills tucked away under wings. Although they breed here, they do so only in very small numbers, and flocks like this are passage birds migrating slowly south.

A wave gently rolls an unremarkable pebble on the sand. The next fails to do so; the next fails to reach it. High tide has passed. The strip of mud between the cord-grass and the waves widens with the ebb. Strings of ringed plovers skim over the sea, their flight slightly jerky with strong downstrokes of their wings, as if they are flicking the air away behind them. As they alight with wet lilting calls, that jerkiness is transferred to their ground movements – they run and stop and wait and bow to peck a food item from the surface of the mud; wait motionless again, as if savouring it or considering pecking again, then run and stop some more. They are joined by a few dunlin, touching down gently from compact flocks with fluid flight, dark legs extended seeking the mud. On land they are also more fluid than the plovers, scampering around, running or walking hurriedly, feverishly pecking at the surface, packed with more urgency than the sedate plovers, always moving, never waiting, fidgeting along the tide's edge like children told to stay still yet not quite able to suppress their energy. Amongst them, four sanderlings are resting on one leg, three now moulted into their winter whites and greys, but one still retaining most of the rufous chestnut that has graced its breeding grounds. They are suddenly dissolved in a rain of dunlin as another flock of several hundred land around them. Although slightly larger and more rotund, they are chased and bullied by the frenetic dunlin, and move to join with a dozen others just landed, seeking solace of their own kind as migrants often do. A large female sparrowhawk cruises low along a glaucous-grassed dune slack, hidden from view from the beach. She flicks over the dune crest, hoping to surprise a skylark, but instead detonates the waders from the edge of the mudflats. With surprise lost and lacking the speed to fly them down in the open, she continues tight in along the dune edge, ignored by the sleeping gulls and shelduck as the waders precipitate back to the shore. The tide recedes, the mud is reincarnated. Straggling flocks of moulting black-headed gulls drift down to it and land. They preen, bright in the sunlight. Smoother, flatter mud is now appearing, and as the wader flocks move out to exploit its food sources more sanderlings appear, running on tiptoes light-footed in and out of the surf, playing chase with the waves.

AUGUST
A FIELD OF DREAMS

The dawn chorus is threadbare now: just the lacklustre trills of a wren, their brightness tarnished, their energy rusted with the passing of time, and the soft rhythmic pumping of the stock doves' flocculent notes, drowsy pulses of cushioned sound drifting away in the morning air. Early chill dissipates as the spectral white glare of sky morphs slowly into a flawless gulf of blue, the ghost of moisture across the distant horizon dissolving in the rising brightness of the dazzling sun. Late hay is dry on the stem in the baked field, a pale rich tawny-blond ahead of its imminent cutting. Slowly the meadow yellows as the multitudes of autumn hawkbit flowers slough off the night's chill and open in the warmth and light. Butterflies still sip at the yellow stars, but many of the heads have exploded into white downy novae, attracting flocks of house sparrows and goldfinches to feed on the seeds. White-tipped bumble bees grope sluggishly across the livid magenta pads of the tall musk thistles intoxicated by the heady nectar within, but these too are now erupting into fluffy white cushions like rabbits' tails. Leaf-beetles feed on the white umbels of upright hedge-parsley, the green armour of their elytra shining in the sun. The grass is full of chains of field bindweed coiling around stems; its white trumpets, spoked with pink, have all unfurled in recent days. Along the track the gravel swallows the gaudy colours of a peacock as the butterfly closes its wings and becomes a black stone in the dust. Swelled by first broods now on the wing, flocks of swallows dive and twist across the tops of the grass, glinting blue. They perch along the house gutters, chittering congenially, pearly breasts bright in the sun's radiance. Amongst them are three sand martins, smaller, more compact, dull brown, with a brown breastband smudged across the purer whiteness of their underparts. They are southbound, but heading temporarily north-east along the coast before resuming a southerly course on the far side of the river, their flight still leisurely, indirect and looping, turning back to chase prey, interweaving briefly with the swallows. There is a sudden spike of intense strident calling as the swallows respond to the shape of a drifting sparrowhawk, hurling needles of sound from angled assaults at the predator like javelins, trying to deflect its progress amongst them. Yet all is in vain, for their vigilance in detecting the hawk has failed this time: it is already clutching the limp bulk of a recent fledgling close to its belly as it rises slowly across the fields.

Heat presses up from the parched grassland, dazzling sunshine burns down savagely from a blue void, the interface melts in shimmering haze; even middle-distance solidity looks unstable. Wind is almost absent, the sweltering mudflats a barrier to any sea breeze reaching this land from the far distant low tide. Only an occasional puff of disturbed air stirs the heat. Dust spirals in small devils from the arid sandy track. A crow berates the torridity. The galaxy of water-crowfoot is dying in the dewpond, its universe shrunk by the ravages of evaporation. It has become a black hole of desolation, the last few imploding white stars of the flowers clinging to the tiny remnants of water; yet these still provide resting places for slender, blue-tailed damselflies. A pair of mallard waddle up from the depths of the drying pond, quacking softly with concern but resisting flight. Any exercise is debilitating. The hot air is thin and oppressive. Oxygen seems scarce. Exertion builds body heat that can barely be shed. Everything is listless; everywhere is still. Only the swallows and insects inhabit the world of angular light and searing brightness; all else seeks the softness of shade. In the bower of long grass where the sunbeams dance in the dappled dimness below the large leaves of the walnut tree, a fox takes respite, lying on its side panting gently, its pink tongue lolling, its jowls marked with grey. It snaps playfully or perhaps in irritation at a passing butterfly. A juvenile robin, its breast still spotted brown, makes occasional sallies from the cool dark caverns between the leaves to snatch unsuspecting insects from the dazzling incandescence outside the tree. A whitethroat churrs from deep in the brambles. Beneath a hawthorn, the fetid stench of sheep rises acridly from the fly-humming shade in which they shelter.

At the point there is a breeze. There is always a breeze at the point, formed from the differential heating of the sea and the river and the land in

196

between, chilling in winter or cooling in summer. Moulting shelduck wait out another day of flightlessness. They line the river's low-water channel across the mud, proximity to water providing slight relief from the heat rising from the dark scorching flats. Others pack into dense flocks on the sand of the point, each identical, sitting head under wing, hovering in the distortion of the haze. Free from tides and free from rain, the midsummer marshes are dry and cracked, the green sward criss-crossed by numerous snaking brown trails, worn by the repeated passage of sheep hooves. They are empty except for sheep which graze reluctantly or lie flat out as if collapsed on their sides or bellies in macabre imitations of death. Skylarks are grounded, their bills held open to dissipate body heat. They flush only from close underfoot amongst the broken shade of the sea couch-grass. All await the respite of nightfall.

Another warm soft-sunny late afternoon; early cloud has drifted east. Families of swallows twitter constantly as they skim insects from the lee of the hedges, flurries of sound occasionally escalating as parents make momentary union with their young to pass them food on the wing. Two months on from a shaping storm, new growth gushes forth from the leeward side of the hawthorns, while the windward side remains brown and crinkled, victim of the salt-laden gales. Skylarks, disturbed by footsteps, zip out of the grass, discarding shiny trinkets of sound. From silvered thistles gone to seed goldfinches tinkle persistently, youngsters' faces not yet flushed red. The burry interrogative of a collared dove's landing note rises into the warmth of the afternoon as it alights in the branches of a willow. The sun is sinking slowly, turning the bleached late summer grass golden as it is tossed gently by the wind. As evening wraps itself slowly around, coddling one's senses in silent and gradually foreshortening greyness, five calves chase a vixen across the short grass of a recently topped pasture. She doesn't seem to appreciate their boisterous inquisitiveness and breaks into a trot just fast enough to evade their playfulness, but then makes a sharp turn through a bramble hedge to cut the encounter short, leaving the calves to return to the more mundane task of grazing. Dunlin titter on the silver line 'twixt the flat dark mud and the incoming evening tide which brings the soughing of the sea; ever the soughing of the sea.

Golden grows the grass, gilded now that summer wanes
Shines briefly in the evening sun 'fore colour drains
From fields and trees now honeyed by the slipping sun,
'Neath which rabbits feed and chase, as the shadows run.

The hay now cut, the stubble green
And wagtails on the hay bales glean
For insects, while the sun rays gleam
Above this evening so serene.

Golden grows the grass, gilded now an ochre haze
Where goldfinches charm thistle tops and pied cows graze
The aftermath, and throaty pigeons' purrings glaze
The cooling air, while gulls fly in the sun's last rays.

Breeze stirs, skies clear, the heavens soar
And curlews bubble from the shore;
The evening sun now gone therefore
Golden grows the grass, no more.

A strange whistling heralds the dreamland of a summer's morning, somewhere between slumber and wakefulness, the clean sheets crisp, the windows flung wide, the warm duvet wrapped against the chill of dawn. As eyes acclimatise to bright light, staring back is a kestrel whose landing wings roused consciousness from sleep. Now perched on the frame of the open window, it is crouched, peering hard with curiosity, round dark eyes liquid and deep and shining. It cocks its head to one side as if a different angle will solve the puzzle of its incomprehension, for humans in bed it has never seen before. It leans further forward and then, distrusting the unknown or fearful of its understanding, it takes flight, curving away out of sight of the bright rectangle of the day, its wings briefly playing the same chords that announced its arrival. The calm of early morning conveys the promise of a gentle summer's day, the air bright with the translucent clarity of religious faith but soon to be sullied by the gathering clouds growing like self-doubt, crowding together, absorbing the light, casting dullness across the fields ahead of an advancing depression.

Late morning, and the air is tropical, thick and heavy and humid, moisture trapped by the pillowed clouds. The sea is liquid brown like gravy where the last of the sunshine seeps through the diminishing gaps of blue. On the rising tide the warm westerly wind has woken white horses from their summer slumber. The reedbed swishes and sways like a sinuous animal stirring ahead of locomotion, a heaving green chimera with the rippling muscles of a giant serpent and a fringe of coarse feathers of aubergine-coloured seed heads. In the late hay meadow, second-brood common blues are on the wing. The sapphire males and dingy brown females both have white-bordered wings. They feed on the tired flowers of bird's foot trefoil and autumn hawkbit, keeping low amongst the sun-bleached grass, sheltering from the wind that tugs at the stems above. Linnets chirrup and goldfinches jingle overhead. With breeding over, both are now nomadic, the flocks flushed with juveniles, searching for seeds. A wall brown basks on the shingle along the edge of the coast path, soaking up the heat retained in the stones and the last dregs of intermittent sunshine, the deep ochre of its wings fractured by the brown lines of its markings. It hugs the deep shelter between the long grasses away from the buffeting breeze, reluctant to fly.

Curlew numbers are rising, migrants adding to the small numbers of non-breeding birds that have remained here throughout the summer.

These may be birds returning to winter in the bay or passage migrants that will head further south; perhaps both. A partial albino is with them, a curious bird with a white head that has been recorded overwintering here for almost twenty years. The birds in the flock are pushed up the shore repeatedly by the advancing tide, their excited conversations rising and falling as they shuffle away from the waves. Finally, they lift into the aurora of their calls already streaming in the air. Fine rain floats on the wind in defiance of gravity. Recent big spring tides have revitalised the saltmarsh; lagoons and pools sparkle silver, full of water. Large flocks of black-headed gulls wait out the high tide amongst them, most of their heads now shot through with white as if beset by old age. Other waders have also returned, the black bellies of the dunlin and the warm rufous of the knots now diluted as they moult toward the Arctic palette of their winter plumage. With the waders have come the first of the winter's peregrines: a heavy-set female cruises the clouds, her bulk as solid as granite, her silhouette as sharp as flint. She turns away from the light, dully lustrous upperparts the colour of gunmetal, throat and neck unblemished white, underparts finely vermiculated with black, all capped by jet-black crown and broad moustachial stripes holding the shining black yolks of her eyes. She flies with measured wingbeats, nonchalant in the wind, circling high above the saltmarsh and the river, inducing angst in a thousand gulls below. She drifts towards the eastern hills, away from the banks of rain dissolving the western horizon. With her departure, the broken promise of a gentle summer's day fragments as gravity begins to crash heavy raindrops to earth in a deluge from the ragged clouds above.

The late hay meadow has been cut. It is like a corpse now, deprived of its soul – soft colours and shifting shades removed, flower heads and seed pods felled and scattered. It has lost communion with the air above, for the swallows no longer swoop through the reflected light of its sward. All is still and lifeless. Haymaking has always been a violent and savage act. Even in earlier times when not mechanised, the scythe still wrought the same effect, yet somehow it has been romanticised through the destructive sparkle of nostalgia. And the smell: that primal sweetness, instantly recognisable, dry and tickly, conjuring warmth and comfort and well-being. Yet the very reason of the meadow's existence is precisely the moment of its death and its subsequent afterlife. Cut, dried, spun into rows, baled and transported away, the vibrance of the summer has been distilled into the musty ambrosia of its fragrance to be unlocked in distant barns to give life to livestock in the dead of winter. And the lateness of its harvest is what sets this meadow apart from others on the peninsula, for the seeds of the wildflowers have had time to ripen and drop. With fertiliser limited to only that from livestock which will graze it through late autumn, the limited nutrients mean that these wildflowers can continue to compete and thrive amongst the more nutrient-demanding grasses and paint the meadow with colour and butterflies next summer.

So the tractor came and cut and spun, and the butterflies sought the dying flowers drying in the sun while overhead swallows twirled and reaped a short-lived bounty, filling the air with their liquid aqueous twitterings even while gorging themselves on the fleeing insects. Thirty to forty yellow wagtails, southbound from the water meadows of England, stopped by, bringing life to the horizontal dying grass, a rhapsody of movement, tripping daintily along the edge of the rows, tails pumping incessantly. Most were immatures, off-white and washed-out brown, with just an intimation of pallid yellow on their rear underparts, but amongst them were a few darker and greener and yellower females and a single male, still adorned in daffodil yellow, fading slightly from the abrasion of a long summer. All were foraging frantically on the bonanza that had been laid before them, fattening up for their southerly journey. A young fox came and watched them, sitting on a warm row near the middle of the field, the sun lifting the scent of drying grass to the sharpness of its black nose. It sat with its tail curled around its paws, panting gently in the heat, its body carrying the leanness of youth, alert and curious, its fur rich and glossy. Its eyes, recently turned brown from the blueness of cubhood, observed the wagtails intently, absorbing, learning. After a while it stood and trotted across the field, stopping abruptly, holding one foreleg off the ground, its tail horizontal like a pointer, ears erect and twitching – then bolted forward, launching itself in an arc through the air. Rabbits watched it from the spoil heaps of their burrows at the edge of the field as it slunk away, disowning its failure to secure a snack. But all has gone with the bales now. Only the frayed cut stems remain, hard and unyielding and jagged underfoot, the aftermath an alien acid green in a landscape of soft-hued alkaline colours. Until the sheep are put to their late autumn grazing, nothing but the rabbits will move here.

Mid-month mellowness, the restiveness of spring has gone, the verdant opulence of summer has passed, the menopause of the year when, just ahead of autumn, hormones slow and satisfaction seems to spread, the land taking on an inward glow that remains even when no sun shines; the soul of late summer. A soft, day with the lightest of drizzle falling like pinpricks on the skin, barely wet, more a breath of heaven; the dark grey clouds welded to the glowing green land by a narrow silver band of light low on the horizon; a day reminiscent of that distant one when we first viewed the Farm. Drifting in and out of the tattered lower edges, a diffuse flock of southbound golden plovers call their ringing plaintive vibratos, a mosaic of laments filling the low clouds with lost memories of the moors now long ago and far behind. An immature herring gull stands statuesque against the sky atop the roof of the black Dutch barn, discombobulating the stock doves whose home has been suddenly invaded. They seem not to know what to make of the gull, trotting around it at a safe distance with short rapid steps of their faded pink legs, peering closely at it from all angles, stretching their necks and tilting their heads as if understanding will come from a new perspective.

In the lane, a chiffchaff flits furtively between the wet foliage of the willows, quivering leaves, kindling sparkles from the raindrops. It is tail-less, having succumbed to the havoc of its annual moult, and remains largely hidden yet never still. It calls repetitively, an insistent single up-slurred whistle, urgent and enquiring. A flock of young goldfinches come to land in the same trees before inexplicably jinking away in bounding flight as if they have touched an electric fence, their constant twittering a chandelier of sound twinkling in the damp air. In the nearby pastures, the first of the field mushrooms are rising, rounded white caps pushing up through the rough grass.

An adumbration skims over them, an insubstantial blur weaving through the willows around the pond, dipping over the garden wall and condensing from the drizzle as a sparrowhawk on to a fence post. On a day of young birds, it is a first-year, underparts white, washed with ochre and with heavy dark tawny barring, its upperparts chocolate with ginger fringes to the feathers and two white fake eye-spots on its nape. It shakes a glaze of rain from its plumage but remains tense, poised on the verge of take-off. It has already inherited the schizophrenia of its existence, fearful yet feared, and torn between the irreconcilable incompatibility of constant motion and the need for occasional rest. Yet even at rest it is as if that constant motion of its body has simply been distilled into its head which continually swivels and bobs, its incendiary eyes searching, ever searching. Is it ever still? Does darkness bring stillness to it during its night-time roost? Perhaps, but even then its dreams are probably full of motion. The slightest of breezes ruffles its breast feathers as it leans forwards, raises its tail and ejects a thin stream of white waste, and immediately slips back into flight low along the emerald latticed arbour of the lane.

Sunshine blazes. Rain hangs from black clouds. Rainbows bloom and wither. A day of heavy showers and light breeze. In the midday brightness, a hobby flickers eloquently over the fields, long primaries bouncing off the air, flight fast and buoyant, interspersed with fluid glides. Although frequent over the wetlands inland, the summer falcon remains uncommon over the peninsula, its appearance always raising the viewer's pulse and eliciting a smile. Swallows flee, hurling the barbs of their alarm calls behind them, but the hobby hasn't come to hunt these today. Instead it jack-knifes abruptly, forward momentum jerking right, wings pumping deeply to redirect it, then left, then right again. It climbs hard, flips over onto its back and stoops from the top of the loop, but unlike a peregrine it continues to flap hard with tail fully fanned to maximise agility. It pulls sharply out of the dive then rises, again twisting upside down and thrusting its yellow feet upwards. Suddenly it is sedate, all urgency drained as it rolls out into a glide and drifts gently to rest on a fence post, having secured its prey. For the peregrine the stoop is the killing manoeuvre in itself, the energy generated from the speed gained being used to kill its prey, either in a dive or in level flight; but for the hobby the stoop enables it to match the velocity of its high-speed and nimble prey, getting it close enough to snatch it from below. It perches on one leg, for in the other it clenches a glittering red dragonfly, knuckles tight, like a child holding an ice cream cone, and dips its head to rip away the four wings that it has just out-flown, discarding them for their last journey on the breeze. Bit by bit the head and body are consumed at a leisurely pace until the bird wipes its bill on the wood as if sharpening a razor on a leather strop. It takes wing once more. Like an outsize swift it cuts through the air, its wings taut and flexing like metallic blades, their blurred motion quivering softly like a flame. It repeats the aerobatics, duelling with a dragonfly until the same outcome is announced by the return of leisurely flight. This time it lifts its prey to its beak and discards the wings while it is still airborne, then planes back to the same post to consume its catch. At rest it is placid, exhibiting none of the febrile excitement so common in other small raptors. Its black eyes are soft and deep. As in flight, it possesses exquisite elegance when perched, its body slender, enhanced by its long primaries overlapping the tip of its tail. It exudes refinement, with slate-blue upperparts, bleached white underparts and pinstripe black breast, a jet-black Hunnic war helmet, the black face-protectors like thick teardrops, and an aristocratic narrow white supercilium, all accented by rufous-orange thighs glowing in the sunlight. It disdains a rattling magpie that perches close, trying to displace it.

It flies once more, catches a dragonfly once more, settles to eat once more; but its meal is cut short. Walkers are on the paths today in white hats and garbed in lurid yellows, pinks and turquoise, the hideous imaginings that designers call fashion. And chatter, always chatter: looking but not seeing, hearing but not listening, their loud discordant voices intrusive and far-carrying, mouthing the inane ramblings of their minds to the wind; walking through a landscape yet not belonging to it. If only they had been shown how to see, and taught the value of silence, for only in the silence will a place offer up its secrets. Nature recoils from their toxicity like grease from detergent; the fox watches warily then slips silently from the field into cover below the brambles; the stoat dashes along the wheel ruts of the lane; the rabbits bounce through the grass to their burrows; the hare freezes then pulls itself even more tightly to the earth; the birds flit through the trees and cease their songs. After they pass, collective breathes will be released, activity and sound washing back into the vacuum, like water in the wake of a ship. But for now, the hobby flickers away unnoticed.

Morning is bright, polished by the early sun. Shadows are sharp. Reed buntings call wistfully in the soft wet air into which the first chill is uncurling like the fronds of an opening fern, nipping at summer's tail. Cattle lie on the damp grass amongst whispers of white mist rising from the overnight rain. They all face outwards in a loose circle, the anachronistic echoes of a pre-domesticated past. Across the channel, great crags of cumulus hang on the horizon like the shattered face of an immense calving glacier. Far away, the high lands of the moor rise blue. That is remote land, never part of this world, the low flat world of the peninsula, always just a backdrop at the edge of perception. A woodpigeon coos its refrain from a sallow by a pond, its throaty crooning vibrating gently in the still air; as it ceases another starts mid-distance, and beyond that yet another, like reflections of reflections running away in opposing mirrors, each dimmer than the one before. A young robin lands on a rusting field gate, the first red breast feathers just starting to displace the spotted brown of juvenile plumage. In the garden, a male blackbird stabs repeatedly at a windfall apple, excavating a white hole beneath the shiny green skin. Large flocks of swallows perch on wires, like quavers on a stave of a score that will never be heard, dreaming now not of England's greener shores but of Africa, chattering convivially as if telling tales of heat and dust to be found soon to the south. Their underparts are pearlescent in the liquid light, the adults' throats ruby, the streamer-less youngsters' sun-bleached terracotta. Then as one they spill from the wires like a sandcastle washed away by an incoming wave, the birds transmuting from sand to wave as they take wing. Rabbits sit on their haunches in the lee of the brambles, enjoying the warmth of late season sun, rays glowing pink through their ears. Families of goldfinches feed on thistle and teasel seeds, all the while twittering appealingly. Dark crimson berries burnish the hawthorns, but the tightly-packed elderberries remain as yet an insipid green. Along the rhynes, sunlight frosts the great willowherb as it filters diffusely around the downy stems and leaves. The last of its cerise flowers sit atop elongated pods bursting with fluffy seeds. The first traces of yellow are just permeating the willow leaves. All around, summer is dying.

As the morning ages, watercolour clouds blotch into the sky, heavy as if they have feasted and are too bloated to move. White sunlight gleams off their rims. From the wet distance of the mudflats, whimbrels witter, the sound like a seamstress's precision sewing machine trying to repair a rip in the air. Their calls are braided with the anguish of the more familiar curlews. Black-headed gulls drift silver over the light running through the reedbed, ever vocal in their castigations. The reeds weave and sway in the drifting breeze, yet in late summer they are green and soft, and the leaves slip past each other frictionless like green silk with just a shimmer of sound: a quality akin to a seashore with distantly breaking waves, just the slightest murmur sliding in and out of earshot – not yet the desiccated tawny stems that will rustle and fret in the winter winds. On the saltmarsh, a plethora of white feathers moulted from shelducks and gulls is concentrated around the edge of a pool like an armada of becalmed skiffs. A small flock of black-tailed godwits feeds languidly in the shallows, the radiance of their breeding plumage as lost as a pensioner's youth, yet their long bills and legs still confer a timeless elegance. Along the rim of dried algae that lines the pool's shore, two svelte greenshanks step sedately, their long legs and slender slightly upturned bills full of genteel charm, the embodiment of understated beauty. They carry the colours of the northern flow country in their plumage like keepsakes; the black centres of their scapulars as dark as the wet peat, the delicate moss-green of their legs like the soft sphagnum, and the dark barring on their white tail like the wind ripples on the bog pools. Disturbed, they take to the air, revealing a long wedge of white along their rump and back, toes trailing tail, long wings bequeathing easy grace, their flight surrounded by a bubble of ringing three-note whistles.

The disturbance is the dredger chugging out downriver on the top of the flood tide, diesel engines throbbing, bow wave heaving through the water. The hull shows rusty red below the Plimsoll line, the empty vessel sitting high in the water, ready for another trip to gouge aggregate from far out on the bed of the channel. Most birds flee its approach in panicked flight, but today not all can do that. Today the river is full of moulting shelduck bobbing in the shelter of its quiet waters, currently flightless. Panic is now for real, since their only means of escaping the monstrous giant is to run through the water – which they do, unseen legs thrashing, muscles straining, webbed feet fanned, forcing the water behind, necks outstretched and wings flapping uselessly at their sides. The dredger slows. A tiny yellow box-like catamaran edges across its bow, then turns about to settle alongside, like a wasp onto the flank of a shire horse. The pilot, who has overseen the big ship's safe passage past the shifting mudbanks of the sinuous river, makes the even more precarious transfer down the swinging ladder to his eponymous craft. The little boat buzzes away to the far shore as the dredger's engines churn and it heaves once more past the point and out into the running tide.

Above the church tower across the river, lilac-grey with distance, the cross of St George hangs limp against its pole. Black-headed gulls appear stranded like flotsam along the top of the gleaming wet river mud. The late August air is sweet and heavy and hot. Trees and bushes are thickly green. Flowers are almost over: only the last yellow of the fleabane and smooth sow-thistle cling on. Gantries of rusting docks rise at the field edges like derelict wharfside cranes. Above them, a blackbird balances amongst the bramble stems, heavy with swelling fruit, testing the first of the ripening blackberries, shiny and enticing yet still sour to the tongue. Amongst the scree of pebbles fallen from an ancient decaying wall, a slowworm has slithered to warm itself amongst the rising heat of the stones. Avoiding direct sunlight, it blinks slowly in the dim shade, where its dull bronze scales exude a faintly burnished sheen. A buzzard has returned to frequent the wooden fence posts, to the annoyance of the local crows whose raw cawing grates against the morning's serenity. The wild airy ringing laughter of herring gulls pervades the echoing air as they straggle across the blue above the house towards the mud.

The day pants, the land dozes, the light is incandescent. The distance is a realm of mirages. The sea seems to have evaporated, now just ribbed mud littered with distorted shelduck. Soporific rabbits lie full length on the sand outside their burrows or sit on mole spoil, licking their paws and washing their ears. Woodpigeons purr drowsily. The only movement is in the tails of the sitting cattle flicking flies and the ever-skimming swallows, or an occasional magpie beating across the pastures. Time drifts. By afternoon, the grasshoppers' softly sonorous rasping is as if the meadow itself is gently snoring. It has become a field of dreams. A zephyr tiptoes through the sweltering garden, tickling the willow leaves, twitching the rabbits' noses, teasing the lethargy with the briefest cool sensual caress – a passing reverie.

August has dreamed by, each day lazy and slow, some with warm sunshine, some with showers, yet all placid and leisurely; now it has dawdled by in a flash and like the instant of youth it is gone. From the mouth of a robin, a soft tic-tic that breaks into a mourning trill – gone the vibrant percolations of spring, instead the first melancholy quavering lament, a broken sad sweet song, serenading summer's senescence, the first breath of autumn folding out of summer. The shimmering time is over; winter … with its winds … cometh.

EPILOGUE
AN OUTSIDER

One day a figure, all alone and unobserved, will walk the fields or paths in the honeyed light of an autumn day, the warm embrace of a summer's evening, the intimate drizzle of a winter's afternoon, or the rising hope of a spring morn. That figure will be someone who I have loved and who loves me still, for they will be carrying my ashes to scatter to the wind of the moment – the wind, the gentle lover and violent partner of this land – perhaps along the coast path that I have trod so many times or in the corner of the field where grows my favourite hawthorn bush. And in that moment, inevitably acid in loss and saddened by farewells, they will know that I will have returned elementally to the place that claimed my heart so many years ago. For although I am an outsider here and just an observer, never having farmed nor shaped the land as those born and bred here have done, nonetheless this land has embraced my soul and with that departed, it is my wish that my body will return to be at one with the land it so loved. Having wandered the wide expanses of the world and seen so many things that relatively few others have been privileged to view, this remains my favourite place; the place that I found the happiness that all of us seek and so few of us are fortunate enough to find. Time here has sat happily on my shoulders; it has given me the space in which to observe and marvel, to wonder and to write.

All places change, it's what places do, and this is no exception. Here, for years, the wildness of the land has been gradually eroding like the thawing of snow, imperceptibly bit by bit until one day it is no longer the place that it was. It is probably still recognisably the same place to the people who lived here fifty or a hundred years ago and yet not what they knew. For us, the higgledy-piggledy Hebridean fences along the entrance to the village are now characterless wooden post-and-rail; sections of the pot-holed track have been repaired with alien grey aggregate; the little owls are no longer present on the peninsula, victims of renovations to outbuildings including our own. The old sheep farmer died a few years back, and with his passing, his intimate knowledge of the pastures and rhynes and gentle hand on the landscape were lost. They were replaced by a heavily mechanised approach, with outsize tractors spreading fertiliser or cutting the hay, and raging flails butchering hedges to splintered stumps, shattering the calm, bludgeoning the land into providing a financial return rather than caressing it to do so. But more recently, this has changed again and the softening touch of environmental stewardship payments has led to a more sympathetic approach with improved hedgerow management and later-cutting of hayfields. Yet nearby, change has been seismic. The buttercup-strewn meadows along the lane have been replaced by a wetland park complete with all-weather tracks for cyclists and a dog-swimming area; new car parks and a proliferation of signs cater for the influx of visitors encouraged by endless entries and sharing on social media; campervans now migrate here in summer. Memorial benches too have appeared, their proliferation in the countryside an affectation inflicted on the rest of us by bereaved relatives wishing to lay claim to landscapes in the name of their deceased loved ones. The management bodies have strived to resolve the conflict inherent in promoting greater public access with safeguarding the needs of wildlife through undisturbed areas for breeding, feeding, and roosting, yet even here dog-walkers refuse to have their access curtailed by the needs of breeding or wintering birds, so they continue to flout fences and signs prohibiting access to the foreshore. Ringed plovers no longer rear their chicks here as a result, their piping calls in summer now a fading memory. Even the holy grail of tranquillity that some visitors seek is being eradicated by their very presence – as elusive as a mirage.

So some of you may come to see this place; it will not be too hard to identify, and confirmation will be easy. But come not and expect to find happiness here in the same way that I have since its cloak may not sit upon you so lightly, for time makes ghosts of every memory and the place as described in the foregoing was nothing more than a blink in the eye of eternity – it was simply 'motion killed in my mind, and preserved in the amber of my memory'.

For me the world is over though the birds remain to sing,
The sunsets will still flame to die, the dawns the light will bring,
The tides will rise and fall each day, the sea will kiss the shore,
But not for me all this to see, for I shall be no more.

This is our last walk, you and me
Across our field towards the sea
'Neath rain or cloud or clear blue sky
This is where we say goodbye

Stop in the corner by the stile
No tears, no tears, just a smile
Now take the urn I ask you please
Release my ashes to the breeze

For this is where I now belong
This place I loved, and with bird song
Surrounding me throughout the day,
This is where my soul will play

Be sad, be sad, but do not cry
For now it is my time to fly
We've lived and loved and laughed and cried
I'll love you past the day I died

And while I shan't be in your bed
You'll hear me whisper in your head
Sweet nothings, and when times are low
I'll laugh with you when cold winds blow

And all the while that you love me
I shall remain, and I will be
Kept within your heart so warm,
I'll be with you come every dawn

So while I fly and you return
Know for your softness I will yearn
And for your gentle hand in mine
I will wait for the rest of time

This is our last walk, me and you
Though only one trail marks the dew
I am still here to comfort you
(and who is to say otherwise)
Goodbye, for now, but not adieu.

ACKNOWLEDGEMENTS

While it was I who wrote the words that you have just finished reading, it was others who made them into the book that you will shortly close. Chief amongst these is my publisher, Keith Whittles, who was the first I made a direct approach to and ultimately was the one who decided to publish. For this, I will be forever grateful. His generosity of spirit coupled with an infectious enthusiasm have meant he has been a real joy to work with. The book has benefited greatly from my editor, Caroline Petherick, whose deft touches and encyclopaedic knowledge of grammar, syntax, and vocabulary have improved my meagre offering beyond anything I had hoped for. Her easy-going charm in making suggestions and changes made working with her a delight. Thank you seems too small a phrase but it comes with heartfelt gratitude. I would also like to thank Kerrie Moncur, who has done such a beautiful job in designing the book and the covers.

Yet Keith and his team were just the final persons in a long chain. Should I thank my Mum and Dad for nurturing my obsession with birds? And my fearsome English teacher, Dennis Heft, also now long departed, who taught me to write some fifty years ago? Perhaps not, yet it seems that I have just done so. After all, without them, this would never have been.

Although the journey to being published has been long and somewhat arduous it has been made possible by the encouragement and enthusiasm of many. First came my long-term friend and publisher-turned-literary agent Ian Drury who, although specialising in military history, affirmed that this book could be published. Geoff Hill, award-winning travel author and editor of the magazine *Microlight Flying*, where I had some flying articles and letters published, provided kind words on an early draft and instilled me with confidence to continue. After a bruising period with a largely unresponsive literary agent sector, I cold-called Stephen Moss, author and lecturer, for his opinion and advice. I could never have envisaged such a warm reception and my thanks here seem little in comparison with the encouragement and practical help and personal introductions he made for me. One of these was to Mark Cocker, and as a first-time author I approached him with some degree of trepidation. I should not have worried. Mark reviewed my work and helped me find a way forward. He provided a forensic analysis of my writing style and book structure, provided supportive criticism to improve the discipline of my writing, and with his wide knowledge of the industry, directed me towards credible publishing possibilities. His kindness is hugely appreciated. Amongst the many publishers who I approached after Keith, but before he made his decision, one stands head and shoulders above the rest for the belief she generated in me at a time when rejections were weighing very heavily. Mireille Harper at Square Peg wrote me the most uplifting emails and also provided many personal recommendations to her friends and colleagues in the industry, and I am extremely grateful to her. Finally, having read an article that Richard Smyth published in December 2020 in *The Fence*, bemoaning the preponderance of nature writing focused on the author rather than the subject, I contacted him as a kindred spirit for his opinion of an excerpt of my work. His incisive and constructive comments helped greatly.

My sincerest thanks go to HarperCollins for the right to reproduce the quote from JA Baker's *The Hill of Summer* as an epigraph to this book and its reproduction at the end of Chapters 1 and 15 as well as the right to reproduce the definition of place from the Collins Dictionary. My thanks are also extended to Woody Allen and Metro Goldwyn Mayer, and Melissa Harrison and Slightly Foxed Magazine, for their permission to use quotes from their work in Chapter 1; and to Jonathan White and Trinity University Press for permission to reproduce the quote from his work in Chapter 2. All photographs are my own, except for that reproduced on page 16. The person who took this image is unknown but likely to have been a member of the Govett family who built and owned the Farm until the 1980s. It was given to us as a gift from the last of that family's line, Clem Govett's, housekeeper, Molly Ford.

The book is dedicated to Jo – Joanna Haxby – my partner and wife for more than forty years. Ever my most exacting critic, she has given me unconditional love for the longest period of my life, and provided unselfish support for me to pursue birds and travel and work in far-flung corners of the world. For this book, she let me have the time and space to write and re-write and to edit and re-edit. We are the opposite in everything we see and do and yet that complementarity has provided an unbreakable bond that makes me look forward to each new day, for she makes each tomorrow the best day of my life.